Archetype
OF THE
Apocalypse

FIGURE O.1

The Limbourg Brothers. *John the Evangelist,* from *Les Très Riches Heures du Duc de Berry.* 1413–1416. Illumination. Musé Condé, Chantilly, France.

About the Frontispiece (Figure 0.1)

John sits upon a stylized desert Isle of Patmos as his last connection to civilization rows away. He is accompanied, nevertheless, by his theological symbol—the eagle—which patiently holds a pen case and ink. John is about to write the Apocalypse and turns, looking upward toward the disturbing sound of three trumpets at his ear: the voice of "one like a Son of man" enthroned in a starry heaven. Four bodiless seraphim whose wings are covered with eyes surround the Lord while the "twenty-four elders" in white robes and crowns have taken their seats in symmetrical choir stalls. Psychologically, the barren ego realm in the lower half of this miniature has been burst in upon by the upper half, the non-ego realm of the unconscious. John's gesture of fear tells us that this is no easy experience (EDITOR).

Archetype
OF THE
Apocalypse

Divine Vengeance, Terrorism, and
the End of the World

EDWARD F. EDINGER

Edited by
George R. Elder

OPEN COURT
Chicago and La Salle

To order books from Open Court, call toll-free 1-800-815-2280.

The cover painting, John Martin's "The Great Day of His Wrath," is reproduced by permission of the Tate Gallery, London/Art Resource, New York.

Open Court Publishing Company is a division of Carus Publishing Company.

Originally published in 1999 as *Archetype of the Apocalypse: A Jungian Study of the Book of Revelation* (ISBN 0-8126-9395-7).

First paperback printing 2002

Printed and bound in the United States of America.

Library of Congress Cataloging-in-Publication Data

Edinger, Edward F.
    Archetype of the Apocalypse : Divine vengeance, terrorism, and the end of the world / Edward F. Edinger : edited by George R. Elder.
        p.   cm.
    Includes bibliographical references and index.
    ISBN 0-8126-9395-7 (hardcover : alk. paper)
    ISBN 0-8126-9316-X (pbk : alk. paper)
    1. Bible. N.T. Revelation—Commentaries. 2. Bible. N.T. Revelation—Psychology. 3. Jungian psychology—Religious aspects—Christianity. I. Elder, George. II. Title.
BS2825.3.E38   1999
228'.06'019—dc21   99-12421
                                                      CIP

Contents

Illustrations

Editor's Preface

This book will challenge the reader to accept a disturbing premise: namely, that the *world as we know it* is coming to an end in the very near future. Although there is a growing literature on this subject from various angles, the author offers little evidence from the world of politics and military conflict and does not address directly the world's economic, social, and technological vulnerabilities; nor does he make here a mere fundamentalist proclamation that "The End is Near," of the sort certain folk make when things are not going their way. Instead, Edward Edinger provides what none of these perspectives—as realistic or intuitively correct as they may be—has found relevant: he offers *psychological* evidence, gleaned from his reading of culture, from his work with patients whose inner processes provide a window onto the undercurrents of our time, and from his own considerable wisdom.

Edinger is following up on the insights of C.G. Jung, the most profound psychologist of the modern era, who wrote concerning the symbolism of the world's end: "The coming of the Antichrist is not just a prophetic prediction—it is an inexorable psychological law."[1] And the point of Edinger's book is that the time for the fulfillment of this law has arrived. Should one weather the storm of the following chapters, one will be rewarded with insight into the meaning of images that have fascinated our culture for two thousand years: the "End of the World" and the "Last Judgment," the "Seventh Seal" and the "Mark of the Beast," the "Whore of Babylon" and the "New Jerusalem." One will be treated along the way to an understanding of the general violence of our time and the specific occasion of the Jewish Holocaust, the resurgence of primitive sexual behavior and the psychological meaning of AIDS.

At the time of his death in July of 1998, shortly after approving this manuscript for publication, Edward F. Edinger was widely considered the dean of Jungian analysts in the United States. He was born in Iowa in 1922, a date he considered significant—as he said in an interview—for reasons that touch upon the topic of this volume. It was only a year after the appearance of William Butler Yeats's great apocalyptic poem, "The Second Coming;" it was the same year that T.S. Eliot published his scathing description of the modern soul in *The Waste Land,* and it was also in 1922 that Oswald Spengler finished his opus, *The Decline of the West.*[2] Perhaps it should not surprise us that eventually Edinger found his conventional career as a physician meaningless, just as he had already found unsatisfying his early upbringing as a Jehovah's Witness. He did find satisfaction in a personal analysis with M. Esther Harding who had worked closely with Jung; and together, he and Harding would become two of the founding members of the C.G. Jung Foundation for Analytical Psychology and the C.G. Jung Institute of New York. After several decades of private practice in New York City and then in Los Angeles, and after the publication of numerous books that plumb the deepest issues of psychology and religion, Edinger offers us here his seventeenth title.

Archetype of the Apocalypse began as a series of ten weekly lectures, of a similar title, delivered at the C.G. Jung Institute of Los Angeles. Beginning January 4th, 1995, they were attended by about fifty persons, analysts in training along with selected members of the community at large. At first glance, this was an entirely new and exciting effort. Jung had taken on the biblical Book of Job and had responded with his *Answer to Job,* but no followers of Jung had embarked upon a similar "psychological exegesis" of scripture which obliges one to consider specific verses and not merely this or that theme. Roughly half of the verses in the Book of Revelation are commented upon here. In a larger perspective, however, Edinger was not breaking new ground for himself. He had long been convinced that Jung's psychological experience had given birth to a new world view: "an entirely new world view which has as its central

principle and supreme value the human psyche with its unique phenomenon of consciousness." By this comment, the author was
explaining why he had written an essay on the nineteenth-century
"sage of Concord," Ralph Waldo Emerson:

> If the new world view is to take its place as a new cultural dominant, a
> long process of reorientation and assimilation is required. Just as
> emergent Christianity required the devoted efforts of generations to
> assimilate the previous Greek learning, so modern psychology will
> gradually assimilate into its own forms and modes of understanding
> the products of human culture that have preceded it. This task I take
> to be the responsibility of the analyst and psychologically informed
> laity of the present and the future.[3]

By the time of the *Archetype of the Apocalypse* lectures, Edward
Edinger had already taken on this responsibility with many impor-
tant works. To indicate his range of accomplishment, there is the
full-length treatment of *Moby-Dick,* by Emerson's contemporary
Herman Melville; a psychological analysis of Greek myth in *The
Eternal Drama;* essays on major themes in the Hebrew Bible in *The
Bible and the Psyche* and on Christian themes in *The Christian
Archetype;* a study of Goethe's *Faust,* and reflections on William
Blake's illustrations for the *Book of Job.*[4] These are all "acts of assim-
ilation," as is this effort to understand psychologically the Book of
Revelation.

Jung, however, introduced a dark note into this creative enterprise of integrating earlier traditions when he wrote:

> The problems which the integration of the unconscious sets modern
> doctors and psychologists can only be solved along the lines traced out
> by history, and the upshot will be a new assimilation of the traditional
> myth. This, however, presupposes the continuity of historical develop-
> ment. Naturally the present tendency to destroy all tradition or render
> it unconscious could interrupt the normal process of development for
> several hundred years and substitute an interlude of barbarism.[5]

Edinger has said that Jung's remark is really a "prediction."[6] And
one cannot help but recall that the transition from classical Greco-

Roman culture to mature Christian institutions did in fact require much blood and confusion, even centuries of what historians call the "Dark Ages." It follows that we can expect something similar. And lest we not feel what that might mean, we have this comment from an interview with the author:

> It seems absolutely inevitable that immense turmoil, convulsive move-ments and eruptions of chaos in vast proportions are in the making so far as the political-historical aspect of mankind is concerned. That, I think, will dwarf the upheaval that took place at the beginning of the Christian era with the gradual disintegration of the Roman empire. That was small potatoes by comparison to what will happen this time.[7]

Yet Edinger believed that this terrible transition in culture (what the poet Yeats called the "rough beast, its hour come round at last") will be bearable *if we understand the meaning* of what is going on.

It is really to this end that the author produced the following chap-ters. No biblical book—with the exception of the Old Testament Book of Daniel—provides a more sustained treatment of the theme of cultural transition than does the New Testament Book of Revelation. Understanding it in modern terms, assimilating it as a psy-chological document, will help us to grasp the unconscious currents of the present, guide our anticipation of the future, and provide the meaning we need to endure the terror of change. Edinger goes fur-ther: he states the hypothesis that if enough people *understand* what is really going on, if enough people internalize the meaning of "Apocalypse" in their own life process, then—according to the sym-bolism of a "saving remnant" in the Book of Revelation itself—the worst of external catastrophe can be softened. That hypothesis places the reader of this book in a crucial position.

I should note, however, that the author's concern for apocalyp-tic issues is not new. Since the second half of Jung's *Answer to Job* deals with Revelation, Edinger had to comment upon it in his own work, *Transformation of the God-Image: An Elucidation of Jung's "Answer to Job"*.[8] And the author was really in the realm of "Apocalypse" in his study of *The New God-Image, Goethe's Faust,* and the seminal essay entitled "The New Myth" in *The Creation of Consciousness*.[9] The tim-ing of these ten lectures on the specific topic of the archetype of the

Apocalypse in early 1995, however, became shockingly apt. Within a month of their delivery, there occurred the nation's worst terrorist attack: the Federal Building in Oklahoma City was bombed by an American possessed by the archetypal idea that the 168 men, women, and children he killed—and the hundreds he wounded—were part of an "evil empire." He killed them also in revenge for the deaths, two years earlier, of eighty persons of an apocalyptic cult killed in a fiery blaze in Waco, Texas. Deeply moved, Edinger wrote to his city's newspaper the following letter, entitled "The Psychology of Terrorism":

> Terrorism is a manifestation of the psyche. It is time we recognized the psyche as an autonomous factor in world affairs.
>
> The psychological root of terrorism is a fanatical resentment—a quasi-psychotic hatred originating in the depths of the archetypal psyche and therefore carried by religious (archetypal) energies. A classic literary example is Melville's *Moby-Dick*. Captain Ahab, with his fanatical hatred of the White Whale, is a paradigm of the modern terrorist.
>
> Articulate terrorists generally express themselves in religious (archetypal) terminology. The enemy is seen as the Principle of Objective Evil (Devil) and the terrorist perceives himself as the "heroic" agent of divine or Objective Justice (God). This is an archetypal inflation of demonic proportions which temporarily grants the individual almost superhuman energy and effectiveness. To deal with terrorism effectively we must *understand* it.
>
> We need a new category to understand this new phenomenon. These individuals are not criminals and are not madmen although they have some qualities of both. Let's call them zealots. Zealots are possessed by transpersonal, archetypal dynamisms deriving from the collective unconscious. Their goal is a collective, not a personal one. The criminal seeks his own personal gain; not so the zealot. In the name of a transpersonal, collective value—a religion, an ethnic or national identity, a "patriotic" vision, etc.—they sacrifice their personal life in the service of their "god." Although idiosyncratic and perverse, this is fundamentally a religious phenomenon that derives from the archetypal, collective unconscious. Sadly, the much-needed knowledge of this level of the psyche is not generally available. For those interested in seeking it, I recommend a serious study of the psychology of C.G. Jung.[10]

As a sign of the times, this letter was not published. Instead, the nation was deluged with mere descriptions of the horror along with biographies of the suspects with hardly a line of print or moment of television dedicated to *understanding* what had happened. The Governor of Oklahoma would say at a memorial service, "We can't understand why it happened"; Billy Graham, Baptist "chaplain" to the nation, had already confessed on national television before a crowd of weeping survivors that he did not know why God allows things like this to happen.[11] Nobody seems to know what is going on, yet Edinger's book bravely tells us.

HISTORICAL NOTE ON THE BIBLICAL TEXT

The Book of Revelation, also called the "Apocalypse of John," opens as follows: "A revelation (*apokalypsis*) of Jesus Christ, which God gave him so that he could tell his servants what is now to take place very soon; he sent his angel to make it known to his servant John" (Rev. 1:1). Sent by God through the celestial Jesus who passed it on through an angel to John, Revelation became the last book in the New Testament canon officially by the fourth century C.E. It was, by its very position, granted something of the honor long accorded Genesis, the first book of the Hebrew Bible. Yet its acceptance by Christians has never been total: the early Marcionites, who were not fond of the Old Testament, found it too Jewish; the spiritually-inclined found its imagery too sensuous and the idea of a "millennium" of banquets and continued propagation offensive. Jerome, the fourth-century scholar responsible for the Latin translation of the Bible, thought the Book of Revelation might better be considered among the apocryphal—not quite canonical—texts, like that of the richly symbolic book of Tobit. There were repeated intelligent assaults upon the tradition that "John," the author of this Apocalypse, was really an unlettered fisherman and favorite disciple of Jesus as well as the presumed author of the theologically sophisticated Gospel of John.

Some of these doubts concerning the Book of Revelation had to do with the historical context of its readers. As with all "apocalypses" (one scholar calls them,"tracts for bad times") there is in this scripture not only a revelation of divine secrets but also a proclamation of a profound crisis.[12] Indeed, it was probably the crisis of the Roman persecution of Christians under Domitian that sparked the composition of this scripture in the early 90s C.E. Similarly, the earlier Book of Daniel was composed during the Maccabean revolt against the oppression of Jews by Antiochus Epiphanes. When the Church was struggling to survive, the Apocalypse of John appealed; but when the Church became an established institution of the reconstituted Holy Roman Empire, John's visions seemed less apt and perhaps merely bizarre. Thus, Jerome could remark that this scripture "has as many mysteries as it does words," while Augustine could decide that the crisis of Revelation was over and that the Church's success was itself the start of a thousand years of utopia ruled by Christ from heaven.[13]

Saint Augustine's idea of history, however, proved unfounded when Christ did not return to earth in the year 1000 C.E. to pronounce a Last Judgment and to establish a new heaven and earth. Indeed, the actual history of Christianity continued through many critical junctures that reminded its adherents of the apocalyptic Beast: the external threat of Islam, the internal threat of heresies, a secular papacy and the splintering effects of the Reformation, the blasphemies of the French Revolution . . . the American Civil War, World Wars I and II. And with each failure in the expectation of the Second Coming of Christ, the Book of Revelation took on new life as a "tract for bad times." Edinger explains in the following chapters that it was the "archetype of the Apocalypse" that periodically became active in our culture's psyche and found itself adequately expressed in the symbols of the Bible's last book. He points out, also, that today this archetype has been "constellated" in an especially powerful way.

In the preparation of this edition, I wish to thank first of all Gregory J. Sova, Ph.D., who attended the ten lectures upon which these chapters are based and who provided the initial transcript of *Archetype of the Apocalypse*. Lacking those pages, produced without the sure knowledge that others would need them, my work would have been much more difficult. I thank Dianne Cordic, Jungian analyst in Los Angeles and former Director of Training at the C.G. Jung Institute of Los Angeles, for providing not only encouragement but also Dr. Edinger's notes from which he lectured. These notes made it possible to check the transcript for accuracy and even to add some materials for which there was not sufficient time in the oral setting. Annmari Ronnberg and Karen Arm of the Archive for Research in Archetypal Symbolism (ARAS), New York, provided me with just the right images of Dr. Edinger's presentation. Susan Greenbaum informed me of the latest research in the scholarly study of Revelation, while Kyle Williams secured the permissions for the many illustrations of the text. I wish also to thank David Ramsay Steele of Open Court for his spirit of cooperation.

Should one compare the author's lectures on tape with what appears here in the book, one will notice at times a marked discrepancy between the two: different sentences, rearrangements of material, additions and subtractions. That is due to the fact that Dr. Edinger and I felt it wise to turn the language appropriate for a public lecture to that more appropriate to a book—losing the spontaneity of oral presentation but gaining a certain formality befitting an interpretation of scripture. And so I am grateful also to Edward F. Edinger not only for the privilege of editing these, his last lectures, but for his full co-operation with the many decisions about style and content that had to be made, his trust in my judgment and kind way of telling me when I was wrong.

Finally, I thank my wife and three daughters for their loving patience.

GEORGE R. ELDER, PH.D.

1 The Grand Final Catastrophe

ARCHETYPE

In this book, we will examine what can be called the "archetype of the Apocalypse" by way of a fairly close psychological study of the Book of Revelation. I will rely primarily upon the New Jerusalem Bible Version because it is a readily available accurate translation; and it provides in footnotes all references to the Hebrew Bible or the Old Testament. As the reader will discover, the New Testament Book of Revelation is loaded with direct quotations from the Old Testament. We will examine this text intensively, rather than review an extensive body of material; and I suggest that the reader consult the scriptures to be discussed prior to reading each chapter here, looking up references found in the biblical footnotes. In doing so, each person can make an important discovery: by becoming involved in a kind of spontaneous amplification process, discovering in consequence what a rich mosaic the Book of Revelation really is. One cannot grasp Revelation by a superficial reading. In many ways, it strikes the modern mind as bizarre and almost unintelligible. But if one applies oneself carefully to it—especially considering the quotations that are embedded in the text—the book begins to reveal itself.

I always pay attention to the titles of other books and, naturally, pay attention to my own. My title here is *Archetype of the Apocalypse.* Let us try to identify each term and ask ourselves first of all: What is an archetype? We may think we know, if we have studied Jungian psychology, yet it does not hurt to be reminded. First of all, an

1

archetype is a *pattern:* a primordial psychic ordering of images that has a collective or generalized quality; it can be understood, therefore, to derive from the collective transpersonal objective psyche—rather than from the personal psyche. That is one aspect of an archetype. The other aspect to which we do not pay quite as much attention—but which does deserve emphasis—is that the archetype is a *dynamic agency:* It is a living organism, a psychic organism that inhabits the collective psyche. And the fact that an archetype is both a pattern and an agency means that any encounter with an archetype will have these two aspects.

As a pattern, we can encounter an archetypal reality and speak about it as an object—an object of our knowledge and understanding. But as a dynamic living agency it appears to us as subject, as an entity like ourselves with intentionality and some semblance of consciousness. Jung refers to this double aspect of archetypes at the beginning of his seminal work *Answer to Job* where he says:

> They are spontaneous phenomena which are not subject to our will, and we are therefore justified in ascribing to them a certain autonomy. They are to be regarded not only as objects but as subjects with laws of their own. . . . If that is considered, we are compelled to treat them as subjects; in other words, we have to admit that they possess spontaneity and purposiveness, or a kind of consciousness and free will.[1]

The reader should keep that in mind as we proceed to analyze the Apocalypse archetype in particular, because it is like all archetypes when they are evoked, constellated, or activated. This archetype of the Apocalypse takes on autonomy and tends to direct whatever is of a psychic nature in its vicinity to line up with its own lines of force.

APOCALYPSE

The other term in the title is "apocalypse." *Apokalypsis* is just the Greek word that was used for the Book of Revelation which is also more simply called the Apocalypse; in general the term means "revelation." But, specifically, it refers to the "uncovering of what has been hidden." The root is the verb *kalypto,* which means "to cover or to hide"; the prefix is the preposition, *apo,* which means "away or from." So, *apokalypsis* means "to take the covering away" from what had been secret or covered—revealing thereby what had previously been invisible. Yet according to general usage, the term "apocalypse" has taken on the larger meaning of the "coming of deity to assert sovereignty"—or the coming of a Messiah to judge, to reward or punish humanity. We have a whole body of literature in antiquity that can be called "apocalyptic" and which grew up around the idea of an Apocalypse. There are a number of Jewish and Christian apocalypses in the extracanonical literature, but certainly the canonical Apocalypse of John—that we are about to study here—is the most famous of that genre.[2]

The main characteristic of apocalyptic literature is that it describes dreams, visions, or journeys to heaven whereby the seer is shown other-worldly secrets and programs of world history that culminate in the "End of the Age." Typically, an apocalypse contains images of a "Last Judgment" with the coming of a "Messiah" or a divine king, who will impose his punishments but then reconstitute things or bring about a "New Order." More particularly, this literature exhibits four chief features: 1) Revelation; 2) Judgment; 3) Destruction or Punishment (as the consequence of Judgment); and then 4) Renewal in a New World.

What I call the Apocalypse archetype underlies all this ancient literature. It is composed of a network of inter-related images—as are all archetypes—making up a complex symbol system. To hint at some of the images that cluster around the archetype, I offer the following chart of interconnections. Its contents are somewhat arbitrary since it is in the nature of an archetypal network that it can extend farther and farther—eventually to encompass the whole collective unconscious. And unless one imposes some sort of limit on the procedure, one will drown in the process. Perhaps this chart can serve, nonetheless, as a road map for our subject matter or as a general overview for the purpose of orientation. Most of the images referred to here I will discuss in some detail in the following chapters (see figure 1.1).

FIGURE 1.1

The Apocalypse Archetype

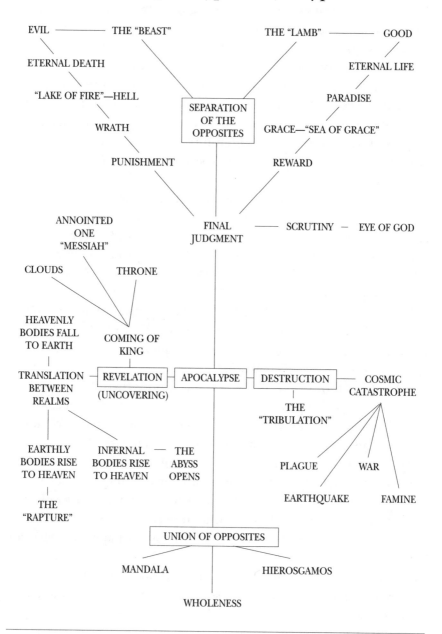

Let me repeat. What we are about to discuss is a primordial psychic pattern of the collective unconscious that is at the same time a dynamic agency with intentionality. When it constellates, it *generates itself* and manifests itself in the individual psyche and the collective psyche of the group it happens to touch. Put differently, archetypes live themselves out in whatever psychic stuff they can appropriate; they are like devouring mouths—finding little egos they can consume, and then living out of those egos. The Apocalypse archetype certainly constellated very powerfully at the beginning of the Christian aeon, and that is why so much apocalyptic literature was generated at that time. Now, again—on the threshold of a new aeon—this same archetype is constellating very powerfully. I will be giving examples of the different ways this is happening today in both the individual and the collective.

Rather than keep the reader in suspense, I will answer the basic question of our study at the outset and then allow the remainder of this work to be an enlargement upon it. The question that really concerns me here is this: What does the "Apocalypse" mean psychologically? My essential answer is: the "Apocalypse" means the momentous event of the coming of the Self into conscious realization. Of course, it manifests itself and is experienced in quite different ways if occurring in the individual psyche or in the collective life of a group; but in either case, it is a momentous event—literally world-shattering. This is what the content of the Apocalypse archetype presents: the shattering of the world as it has been, followed by its reconstitution.

In terms of collective phenomena, we have evidence all around us in our daily analytic practice and in contemporary world history that this earth-shaking archetypal event is taking place right here and now. It has already started. It is manifesting itself in international relations; in the breakdown of the social structures of Western civilization; in political, ethnic, and religious groupings; as well as within the psyches of individuals. One can perceive the Apocalypse archetype active in all these arenas—once one is familiar with its contents and has the eyes to see. One can see further evidence in books, movies, and television programs. The possible encounter with extraterrestrial intelligence is an image that is more and more gripping the modern mind; and in many cases in science fiction these encounters are followed by apocalyptic consequences—an aspect of the archetype.[3]

One can see the archetype of the Apocalypse in the proliferation of apocalyptic cults or sects. And when we consider the phenomenon of religious groups that are quite explicitly identified with this archetype, and not just marginally so, I see a whole spectrum. At one extreme there are the apocalyptic cults of a semi-suicidal nature that are often no more than large family groupings centered around a charismatic character who is quasi-criminal or quasi-psychotic (or both)—such figures as Charles Manson, Jim Jones, or David Koresh.[4] These cults are extreme versions of group possession, concrete group possession by the Apocalypse archetype. A little less extreme but still far out along the spectrum are the bomb-shelter, stockpiling, survivalist cults who are holing up in remote regions—heavily armed and waiting for Armageddon.[5]

Farther along the spectrum are the apocalyptic sects of a larger scale. Let me note that the only difference between a cult, a sect, and a denomination is numerical. A small group is considered to be a cult; a religious group of five hundred thousand to a million members is a sect; and if there are ten million members, that is a denomination—basically, there is no other difference. Of course, the larger the grouping, the more religious issues get ironed out or, shall we say, the fire gets damped down. Now, there are several of these larger apocalyptic sects, but probably the most well-known are the Jehovah's Witnesses and the Seventh Day Adventists. They each have between seven hundred fifty thousand and a million members in the United States alone, with world-wide connections as well.   And they are becoming almost conventional just by virtue of their statistics.[6]

Still farther along the spectrum of apocalyptic groups are the relatively more moderate and even conventional fundamentalist churches who are convinced that the time of the "End" is upon us. Fifty years ago, when I first began to observe this phenomenon, mainstream Christian Fundamentalism did not have such a prominent apocalyptic tone. But today there are millions of Americans who are expecting to be "raptured" up to heaven at any moment. There are millions of Americans who have these convictions.

Finally, at the other end of the spectrum of possession by the Apocalypse archetype are the apparently secular rationalistic environmentalists. I do not mean merely people who are concerned about the environment, I mean those whose behavior and way of life indicate that they are functioning out of a religious dimension of their libido. It is always the passionate intensity that reveals possession by an archetype. So, one does not even have to be consciously "religious" to be possessed by the sacred power of archetypal reality.

In addition to these collective manifestations of the Apocalypse archetype, we have *individual* manifestations which therapists are in a position to see all the time. When the imagery of the Apocalypse archetype comes up in analysis, it can be immediately recognized as part of the phenomenology of the individuation process: representing in an individual the emergence of the Self into conscious realization. And those four aspects that I mentioned earlier with regard to apocalyptic literature apply also to an individual manifestation: Revelation, Judgment, Destruction or Punishment, and a New World. Here, 1) "Revelation" has the psychological correlate of a shattering new insight accompanied by the flow of transpersonal images into consciousness. 2) "Judgment" is experienced in the form of an abrupt profound awareness of the shadow, which at times can be so overpowering that it can threaten complete demoralization.[7] When someone is confronted with his dark and dubious nature that he has known only abstractly and intellectually, but then suddenly it comes into focus as living concrete reality—that is a big shock. 3) The theme of "Destruction or Punishment" is manifested as the individual's anxiety in the midst of this transformation ordeal. 4) Finally, the coming of a "New World" corresponds to the emergence of mandala and quaternity images within the psyche— as there begins to appear the possibility of a conscious relation to the Self and its wholeness.[8]

INTRODUCTION TO THE BOOK OF REVELATION

The Apocalypse or Revelation to John, the final book of the Jewish-Christian Bible, is really an amalgamation of Jewish and Christian apocalyptic imagery and only semi-Christian; it is as though the basic imagery of this literary apocalypse—which derives from other Jewish apocalyptic material—has had "plastered" onto it the image of Christ. It makes repeated references, for instance, to the Old Testament prophecies of the "Great Day of Yahweh." But as the culmination of the Hebrew-Christian canon, it lays out the final scenario of the Christian aeon and describes symbolically the concluding events of the Judeo-Christian myth—a myth that has been the womb and the metaphysical container of Western civilization. So it is no small thing we are examining here.

An immense amount of scholarly work by biblical scholars has gone into the study of this text. Practically all of these scholars, however, have been contained in the myth itself: so they have been trying to understand their own mythological container. As a depth psychologist, I find it very interesting to observe how individuals come to intellectual terms with mythological texts in which they are still contained. There is, quite frankly, a lot of twisting and squirming; for the problem is a bit like that of fish trying to understand the properties of water—the medium by which they are surrounded. Yet it is not really possible to understand or to perceive the subject as an object until one is outside of it; one has to get outside of the container before that becomes possible.

In general, scholars have divided themselves into four main camps, holding four main views about how to understand Revelation. I will not discuss the matter in detail; but, most likely, what we have here is evidence of temperamental variations—typological variations among the scholars themselves.[9] 1) One group holds what has been called a "preterist" interpretation—from the Latin word *praeter,* meaning "beyond or past." And, according to that view, the Book of Revelation is a picture of current events in the Roman Empire that were taking place or had just taken place in the recent past. Therefore, the contents are not prophetic at all; they put into symbolic form that which has already taken place, *praeter.* 2) The second viewpoint is called "historical." It interprets Revelation as a symbolic representation of the entire course of Church history leading up to the final consummation. 3) The third group is called the "futurist" interpretation. According to this view, the text of Revelation refers to events around the Return of Christ, coming sometime in the future. (4) Finally, we have the "idealistic" or symbolic viewpoint. This scholarly viewpoint considers the Book of Revelation to refer symbolically to the "conflict of good and evil" in any age, at any time, and is not specifically or literally historical. One could call this the Platonic view of Revelation.

Looking at the text psychologically, I would set up a somewhat different set of interpretative categories. We might see the text as a manifestation of the Apocalypse archetype—which can express itself in the Book of Revelation in different contexts that overlap and interpenetrate one another. To be more specific, I detect different strands of contextual reference running throughout the tapestry of this book. 1) One of the strands is a description of "past" concrete events in the sacred history of Israel—with the outstanding example being the Babylonian Exile in 586 B.C.E. That was a collective experience of an "Apocalypse" for Israel if ever there was one. And many of the Old Testament quotations embedded in Revelation refer to that incredible event that miraculously did not destroy the nation—it is indeed a miracle that Israel survived. 2) A second strand refers to "present" concrete events; and by present I mean first century C.E. This view corresponds to the "preterist" position which refers chiefly to the destruction of Israel and its temple in the year 70 C.E. by Rome and anticipates the Roman Empire's destruction by divine wrath. 3) A third strand would be a description of "future" concrete events—"End of the Age" events occurring, actually, in our own time. We, of course, are in a position to witness our own contemporary events and can see how a good bit of this imagery fits. Retrospectively, anyway, we can see that strand in the text.[10] 4) Yet another level would be what I would call—to use a religious term—the "eschatological" strand; but to use a slightly more psychological term, we could also call it the "pleromatic" strand. By this I mean that the Book of Revelation refers also to events entirely outside of time that are taking place in the eternal or pleromatic realm of the psyche. In other words, they take place in the collective unconscious and do not necessarily even register at the level of ego consciousness.[11] In fact, to the extent that it is pure archetype and does not descend or rise into incarnation, archetypal reality behaves in that fashion, as an eternal drama that is going on all the time. 5) Finally, the truly "psychological" strand is probably the most important category of all for our understanding of this text: namely, a symbolic expression of the coming of the Self into conscious realization in an individual psyche.

The Book of Revelation is undoubtedly based on a personal visionary experience. But, as I have indicated, it is just as obvious that the text—as we have it—has been influenced by other apocalyptic literature, frequently with direct quotations from that literature. The parallels with Ezekiel's vision are very striking; there are direct quotations from the Book of Daniel. In addition, the scholar R.H. Charles has pointed out at least twenty parallels (if not actual quotations) from the noncanonical Book of Enoch.[12] It is evident that Revelation is a product of assimilation of one kind or another.

There are at least two possible ways to understand how this product may have come about; indeed, there may have been a mixture of the two. One possibility is that the original experience of one individual was taken up by others who edited and amplified it out of their knowledge of other literature. The other possibility is that the Book of Revelation may have been written—in the main, anyway—somewhat in the fashion that the alchemical treatise *Aurora Consurgens* was written. That is a work attributed by some to the medieval theologian Thomas Aquinas—published recently, with psychological commentary, by Marie-Louise von Franz.[13] It is a treatise that integrates biblical imagery, especially the Song of Songs, with the alchemical process; yet it is evident from the way the text presents itself that there was no cool calm editor at work piecing things together. Instead, the *Aurora Consurgens* was composed out of the heat of a living experience, out of the mind of someone for whom the biblical imagery and quotations were such living presences that they became the apt expression of the experience he was having. This could quite possibly be the case with John. We have no way of knowing for certain, but we can feel confident that John's composition is an assimilation product. In addition to assimilating Jewish apocalyptic to the Christian world view, it even incorporates—as we shall see—a piece of classical Greek mythology.

I emphasize this matter of assimilation because it is an important one for psychology. Jung has said in *Mysterium Coniunctionis:* "Any renewal not deeply rooted in the best spiritual tradition is ephemeral."[14] Therefore, Jungian psychologists know or ought to know that the analytic process must be related to the archetypal historical dimension behind the personal experiences of an analysand—if the analysis is to achieve its full depth and effectiveness. The net result of that kind of psychological work is also an assimilation product.

While the author of the Book of Revelation calls himself "John," his identity is not certain. J.M. Ford, in her Anchor Bible commentary, suggests that he is John the Baptist—not a very popular view but one that shows how far some biblicists can go.[15] Traditionally, "John" is the Evangelist—a disciple of Jesus to whom is attributed the Gospel of John and at least the first and second Letters of John. Now, for our purposes, the "tradition" is a psychic fact. It posits the *consensus omnium*, so to speak; it is a statement of the collective psyche and, therefore, has to be taken as a psychic fact at least on one level. Here is what Jung has to say on the subject of the authorship of Revelation:

> One could hardly imagine a more suitable personality for the John of the Apocalypse than the author of the Epistles of John. It was he who declared that God is light and that "in him is no darkness at all." . . . The Father has bestowed his great love upon us . . . . He who is begotten by God commits no sin. . . . John then preaches the message of love. God himself is love; perfect love casteth out fear. . . . He talks as if he knew not only a sinless state but also a perfect love, unlike Paul, who was not lacking in the necessary self-reflection. . . . Under these circumstances a counterposition is bound to grow up in the unconscious, which can then irrupt into consciousness in the form of a revelation . . . . [which] compensates the one-sidedness of an individual consciousness.[16]

Jung is taking the position that the author of the Johannine Epistles is the same as the author of the Apocalypse—if not also of the Gospel—and is stating that the violence of the later visions compensates John's earlier one-sided conscious emphasis on light and goodness. That means John's personal psychology was one factor in the experience. But Jung goes on to say:

> Let us be psychologically correct, however: it is not the conscious mind of John that thinks up these fantasies, they come to him in a violent "revelation." . . . he is a passionately religious person with an otherwise well-ordered psyche. But he must have an intensive relationship to God which lays him open to an invasion far transcending anything personal. The really religious person, in whom the capacity for an unusual extension of consciousness is inborn, must be prepared for such dangers.
>
> The purpose of the apocalyptic visions is not to tell John, as an ordinary human being, how much shadow he hides beneath his luminous nature, but to open the seer's eye to the immensity of God, for he who loves God will know God. We can say that just because John loved God and did his best to love his fellows also, this "gnosis," this knowledge of God, struck him.[17]

In psychological terms, we could say that John's visions opened up his eyes to the immensity of the collective unconscious. An understanding of his personal psychology, therefore, is totally inadequate for explaining the content nature of this imagery. Taken as a whole, the Book of Revelation is a symbolic representation of an encounter with the activated collective unconscious, out of which comes a manifestation of the Self—symbolized in the final chapter of the text by the "New Jerusalem." Since the Self is manifesting itself again in an emphatic way today, it is not surprising that modern dreams often have imagery that is strikingly parallel to that found in the Apocalypse of John.

Now, the word "apocalypse" has come to mean more than the "revelation of things secret." It has come to mean catastrophe. Indeed, a "grand final catastrophe" is now a deeply-ingrained part of the usage of that word. And I think that is the correct and appropriate way of seeing it in all collective manifestations of the archetype; because collective manifestations of the archetype are by definition *unconscious* manifestations of the archetype acted out concretely. When this archetype is experienced by the individual, however, it is not always by any means experienced in the form of catastrophe. To be sure, the coming of the Self is always an upheaval; but this feature is often overshadowed by its positive consequence—the coming of an enlargement of the personality and the emerging relation to the transpersonal level of the psyche. Considering an individual's experience of the archetype, the "Apocalypse" bodes catastrophe *only* for the stubbornly rationalistic, secular ego that refuses to grant the existence of a greater psychic authority than itself. Since it cannot bend, it has to break. Thus, "end-of the-world dreams" (invasion from outer space, nuclear bombs) do not necessarily presage psychic catastrophe for the dreamer but may, if properly understood, refer to the coming into visibility of manifestations of the Self—the nucleus of the psyche—and present the opportunity for an enlargement of personality.

Jung is saying something similar in *Mysterium Coniunctionis,* referring to the image of an earthquake in an alchemical text: "This image tells us that the widening of consciousness is at first upheaval and darkness, then a broadening out of man to the whole man."[18] He speaks in the same regard in his essay *Concerning Rebirth* where we find a quite important statement which I discuss in *Ego and Archetype.* Jung writes:

> When the summit of life is reached, when the bud unfolds and from the lesser the greater emerges, then, as Nietzsche says, "One becomes Two," and the greater figure, which one always was but which remained invisible, appears to the lesser personality with the force of a revelation. He who is truly and hopelessly little will always drag the revelation of the greater down to the level of his littleness, and will never understand that the day of judgment for his littleness has dawned. But the man who is inwardly great will know that the long expected friend of his soul, the immortal one, has now really come, "to lead captivity captive"; that is, to seize hold of him by whom this immortal had always been confined and held prisoner, and to make his life flow into that greater life—a moment of deadliest peril![19]

The point is that if we understand the image of the "Apocalypse" —when we see it in its manifestation, both inner and outer—we do not have to be overcome by it or possessed by it. It is awesome, to be sure, but it is humanized by being understood. In my opinion, as our world sinks more and more into possession by this archetype, nothing is more important than the existence of a certain number of individuals who understand what is going on.

2 Revelation: Chapters 1, 2, 3

THE VISION OF THE NUMINOSUM

Let us begin our study of Revelation proper with chapter one, verse nine, following the introductory address and author's formal greeting:

> I, John, your brother and partner in hardships, in the kingdom and in perseverance in Jesus, was on the island of Patmos on account of the Word of God and of witness to Jesus; it was the Lord's Day and I was in ecstasy, and I heard a loud voice behind me, like the sound of a trumpet, saying, "Write down in a book all that you see, and send it to the seven churches of Ephesus, Smyrna, Pergamum, Thyatira, Sardis, Philadelphia and Laodicea." (Rev. 1:9–11)

This opening scene—the setting for what is to come—describes an experience of the numinosum.[1] We learn that John is on the prison island of Patmos, which is significant psychologically if we consider the experience of imprisonment both objectively and subjectively. For it amounts to having severe restrictions imposed on one's natural libido flow: there is narrow confinement, restriction, limitation. And if we consider the experience not only as a physical event but also as something that can happen psychologically, then we can imagine being "imprisoned" by a very narrow, confining, life- attitude or by one's neurotic complexes. Sometimes complexes are so severe that a person cannot even go out of the house.

So, right here at the beginning of the scripture, there is the image of "imprisonment." The net result of that condition psychologically is a build-up of libido which is not permitted its normal, natural, spontaneous discharge. When this happens, the energy can reach explosive proportions; and, indeed, the eruption of the numinosum is a psychological explosion. The Book of Revelation is itself a psychological explosion. There are real fireworks, cosmic fireworks, in it! Indeed, Revelation is an energy phenomenon. And imprisonment, especially in the symbolic sense, is generally a precondition for such an explosion. That happens in our actual prisons, too; if the libido in a collectivity gets pent up too long, then it has to explode in a riot.

Characteristically, John's attention is drawn to a "voice" that he hears coming from "behind" him; that means the voice is coming from the unconscious. Since he feels obliged to turn around to face it, he is obliged—psychologically speaking—to pay attention to the unconscious. Ordinarily, when we are just going about our usual activities, we do not pay attention to the unconscious: it is "behind" us, and the outer world is in "front" of us. But if something goes on behind us (meaning: from within) that gets our attention, then we have to turn around. That is what happens with John—and that is what the analytic process does. It is a deliberate "turning around" to look at what is behind one, on the assumption that it can be helpful to know what is going on "back there" or within ourselves.

Analysis, however, goes farther than John does. It does more than just turn around and listen; because it proceeds to the next step and tries to promote a "dialogue" between the ego and the unconscious. There is no dialogue in the Book of Revelation, just a one-way communication—a voice that makes the announcements, and a listener. This is what we would call a visionary or a mystical experience, a "one-way" experience; it is passive imagination—not active imagination—and one should be careful to make the distinction.[2] It is, nevertheless, what mystics of all ages strive for. Characteristically, they deliberately and voluntarily generate "prison conditions" within their psyches by fasting, by solitude, and similar procedures. This causes libido to be stored up in the unconscious which, under certain circumstances, erupts into a visionary experience. All "vision quests" do the same thing. In order to develop the libido to create the vision, that energy has to be stored up in one way or another. It then becomes available for the unconscious which can use it to "erupt."

Then the visionary gets a glimpse into the transpersonal psyche, into the collective unconscious. And this experience will be formulated according to the religious conceptions by which the mystic is living; the mystic will have a whole set of symbolic images by which the experience will be interpreted. It can vary, but basically this is the experience of what we call the collective unconscious. Again, characteristically, the experiences are given the highest value by those experiencing them and are considered very valuable for the individual's life. But, I repeat, they are not active imagination and not part of the process of individuation. Individuation requires an active ego participation in the dialogue—between listener and voice—and then assimilation of the contents that are transferred from one level to another. Mystical visionary experience is something different and gives one merely a glimpse.

John, the visionary of Revelation, "turns around;" and this is what he sees:

> I saw seven golden lamp-stands and, in the middle of them, one like a Son of man, dressed in a long robe tied at the waist with a belt of gold. His head and his hair were white with the whiteness of wool, like snow, his eyes like a burning flame, his feet like burnished bronze when it has been refined in a furnace, and his voice like the sound of the ocean. In his right hand he was holding seven stars, out of his mouth came a sharp sword, double-edged, and his face was like the sun shining with all its force. (1:12–16)

The great Renaissance artist Albrecht Dürer produced, as part of his series on the Apocalypse, a woodcut of this very scripture reproduced here (see figure 2.1).

This vision of the numinosum contains such a wealth of imagery that I must choose, more or less arbitrarily, a limited number of features. The "seven golden lamp-stands" is one of the first things John sees. Zechariah, the Old Testament prophet, also had a vision of a lamp-stand with seven lights; and he was told by an angel that these

FIGURE 2.1

Albrecht Dürer. *Vision of the Seven Candlesticks.* ca. 1497–1498. Woodcut.

seven lights were the "eyes of Yahweh" which range throughout the earth.[3] We also know that Yahweh—while giving his instructions for the building of the ark, the tabernacle, and its furnishings— ordered a lamp-stand with seven lamps on it. What John sees, then, is the "heavenly original," so to speak, of the earthly lamp-stand or menorah that stood in the tabernacle; and, as we proceed, we shall find that all the various features of the tabernacle (including the ark of the Covenant) have their heavenly origins revealed in this vision. It is as though we are seeing a Platonic original of the earthly features of the tabernacle.

As Zechariah informs us, these seven lights correspond to the "seven eyes" of God which "range over the whole world." In *Answer to Job,* Jung himself refers to this image. He had been speaking of the fact that at the beginning of the biblical Book of Job Satan appeared in heaven after roaming over the earth; and Jung comments that "Satan is presumably one of God's eyes" roaming the world (along with the other lights in the divine lamp-stand) watching what is going on.[4] This brings up the rich symbolism of the "eye of God," which we will have occasion to discuss below. But here we note that there is a "watching process" going on at the beginning of Revelation—a watching directed toward the ego.

Incidentally, this "sevenfold lamp-stand" (along with the "seven stars" in this part of the vision) will also be a reference to the "seven planetary spirits." Indeed, we are going to hear a lot of the number seven in this book of the Bible. One could say that the Book of Revelation describes a repeated assault of the "Seven" archetype; it is really astonishing how many times the earth gets hit with "seven," the significance of which we will take up later.

A second important image is a figure "like a Son of man." It is a direct quotation from a vision in Daniel which was recorded about 165 B.C.E.; but the image itself first appears in Ezekiel written about 575 B.C.E. In fact, the prophet Ezekiel himself was called the "Son of man." The phrase appears again around 100 B.C.E. in the Book of Enoch, a noncanonical text; early copies of the canon included Enoch which almost made the official cut. And then, as Jung makes clear, Christ was probably thoroughly identified with the "Son of man" image as depicted in the Book of Enoch. He overtly identified

with the term, calling himself "Son of man" around 30 C.E. Since the
Book of Revelation was written about 95 C.E., we can observe in this
chronology the historical sweep of this particular term. Jung interprets the sequence thus: Yahweh was gradually drawing closer to
man by presenting a Messianic figure, labeled the "Son of man,"
who could partake of his own divine nature.

What makes this so important psychologically (of more than
antiquarian interest and worth our serious attention) is that these
data help us reach the conclusion that the realized Self is the "Son"
of the ego or "man." One finds the same notion in alchemy. There,
the Philosophers' Stone—the ultimate supreme goal of the alchemical opus—is called the *filius philosophorum,* "son of the philosophers," in other words, son or product of the alchemists. That
means that the supreme psychological goal has not only a divine
archetypal begetting but also has an earthly ego begetting. Or, to
put it in Jung's lapidary phrase, "God needs man." All of that is
implied in the imagery of the "Son of man."

Another feature of John's experience of the numinosum is "brilliant light." Everything is white, all the way up to the countenance
that was shining with all the force of the sun—with brilliant, brilliant light. So what we have here is an image of "Sol" or the Sun as
the Self. That brings up a question: How can an image represent the
Self, the totality, while picturing only one side of a pair of opposites?
For in this case, the solar attributes are greatly emphasized while the
dark lunar side does not appear. We get plenty of darkness later in
the Book of Revelation, I grant you, but this image is on the face of
it one-sided. I think we can consider it, nonetheless, a genuine symbol of the Self because—to begin with—it does have many features
of wholeness. The Son of man, we are told, is the "First and the
Last" meaning that it has cosmic proportions (Rev. 1:17).

One way to answer the question I have posed is to understand
that the manifestation of the Self is always local. It is, therefore, usually modified to some extent by the nature of the local conditions
of the ego experiencing it—namely, the level of development of
that ego. The degree of one-sidedness of that ego will affect the way
the Self manifests. Certainly, in mystical experience, "brilliant light"
is a very common feature of the vision much as in Revelation. Also

very typical of mystical experience is that it is preceded by a "dark night of the soul." It is as though the emphasis on light or brightness is carrying a *compensatory* aspect for an excessive darkness that the ego is experiencing. Now, in John's case, he was the harbinger of a new aeon and a whole new revelation which was going to bring "light" to the "darkness" of paganism: And that may be another reason for the disproportionate emphasis on light. Beyond that, however, there is the fact that the Christian attitude itself—as it evolved—identified with the "light" and banished the "darkness" as much as possible.

Another feature of this image is the "sharp sword coming out of the mouth." One might consider this image to be evidence of the vision's originality, but that is not the case. In Isaiah, the servant of Yahweh says: "Yahweh called me when I was in the womb, before my birth he had pronounced my name. He made my mouth like a sharp sword" (49:1–2). The author of the Apocalypse is absolutely steeped in Isaiah, not to mention the many other books of the Bible. But the fact that an Old Testament reference is present does not entirely remove the possibility that the image was a content of John's own vision; it only softens its originality. In the image, two different motifs are welded together: the "mouth" and "sword," and they both have the same archetypal reference, namely, Logos. That is the "sharp" thing that comes out of the mouth: the Word. I remind you that it was "John" who equated Logos with God in the first chapter of the Gospel of John; and this connection is made only in his writings. So, here is a good argument in favor of the Evangelist's authorship of the Book of Revelation.

Certain sayings of Christ identify him with the "sword." For instance, Matthew 10:34–36 reads:

> Do not suppose that I have come to bring peace to the earth: it is not peace that I have come to bring, but a sword. For I have come to set son against father, daughter against mother, daughter-in-law against mother-in-law; a person's enemies will be the members of his own household.

This is an image of what the alchemists called *separatio*.[5] Psychologically, it is an image of the discriminating process of consciousness that "cuts up" the state of *participation mystique* keeping one contained in—to change the image—a collective "soup." The Christian aeon was really poised to initiate a vast *separatio* process to which this "sword coming out of the mouth" alludes. Spirit and matter were about to be torn apart violently.

I think we have to understand that historical event to be a developmental requirement of the age: a *separatio* of the unconscious composite had to take place in a decisive way if there was to be the possibility of an authentic *coniunctio*. And I think these reflections are alluded to by the "sword in the mouth." It is an image that may come to mind when one encounters sword dreams which are not uncommon, although today one does not see swords in dreams so often as a pair of scissors, a kitchen knife, or some other kind of blade.

THE SEVEN STARS AND ANGELS OF THE SEVEN CHURCHES

Then we are told that the "seven stars" that are in the mysterious figure's hand are the "angels of the seven churches." In fact, the seven stars, the seven lamps, the seven angels, and seven churches are essentially all the same: the same thing manifested at different levels. The "Son of man" himself states:

> "The secret of the seven stars you have seen in my right hand, and of the seven golden lamp-stands, is this: the seven stars are the angels of the seven churches, and the seven lamp-stands are the seven churches themselves." (Rev. 1:20)

John is instructed to write letters to the "angels" of the seven churches, whose geographical location in the ancient world constituted a sort of circle in Asia Minor. And they are mentioned by John in clockwise fashion beginning with Ephesus and ending with Laodicea (see figure 2.2).

Now, it is quite interesting that John is being told to address his correspondence to these "angels" of the seven churches rather than to the churches directly. What could that mean? Some biblical

FIGURE 2.2

scholars interpret these "angels" as symbols of the "corporate personalities" of the churches which is probably not far from the mark,
if one takes that phrase quite seriously. I think we have here an allusion to a subject that depth psychology has not even begun to
explore. But here is a thought: I believe these "angels" of the seven
churches refer to personifications of collective groupings—yet having a depth connection as indicated by their going all the way back
to the "stars" in the hand of the apocalyptic Christ.

One can discriminate, albeit somewhat arbitrarily, different lay-
ers in the collective unconscious. Moving downward, the first level
of the collective unconscious is the family ancestral layer; the next
level would be the national layer; followed by the ethnic-tribal layer
which is older and more primitive than the national; then on down
to the animal layer; and eventually to the vegetable; and finally the
inorganic layer at the bottom.[6] As I see it, each of these functioning

groups has a "collective soul" symbolized by either an "angel" or a "demon"—essentially the same intangible psychic dynamism but attached to either a positive or negative sign.

Now, when an individual is living in a state of *participation mystique* with a group, the "collective soul" of that group is that person's *spiritus rector* or guiding light. I think it is to this phenomenon that the scripture alludes by the image of the "angels of the seven churches." But, as I have indicated, their collective souls are rooted in a psychic depth that does not derive from their concrete coming together. If a group of individuals of like mind come together and form a group, a "group soul" is almost always constituted to some extent; it may be, however, a very superficial group soul. On the other hand, if the group soul corresponds to one of the "stars" in the hand of the deity or to one of the "lights" in the divine lampstand, that means what has been constellated derives from far greater depths than the actions of the individuals who make up the group.

I am going into this matter at some length for the reason that Jungian psychology has a real contribution to make in the creation of an "archetypal group psychology," a psychological field which does not yet exist. Von Franz, however, describes quite nicely the ideal psychological group in her work, *Projection and Re-Collection in Jungian Psychology:*

> [B]onds with other people are produced by the Self and these relations are very exactly regulated as to distance and closeness. One might describe this as the social function of the Self. Each person gathers around him his own "soul family," a group of people not created by accident or by mere egoistic motivation but rather through a deeper, more essential spiritual interest or concern: reciprocal individuation. Whereas relations based merely on projection are characterized by fascination and magical dependence, this kind of relationship, by way of the Self, has something strictly objective, strangely transpersonal about it. It gives rise to a feeling of immediate, timeless "being together." The usual bond of feeling, says Jung elsewhere, always contains projections that have to be withdrawn if one is to attain to oneself and to objectivity. "Objective cognition lies hidden behind the attraction of the emotional relationship; it seems

to be the central secret." [7] In this world created by the Self we meet all those many to whom we belong, whose hearts we touch; here "there is no distance, but immediate presence." [8]

I have diagrammed this "ideal group" to try to make the matter clearer (see figure 2.3). In this setting, each individual (represented by the little circles) has established his or her own conscious relationship to the Self (the large circle). Therefore, the relationship that each has with the others in the group is really a shared experience of that psychological achievement. Here, the "corporate soul"—the collective experience shared jointly—has been adequately mediated by each individual so that it is indeed a "guiding angel." The crucial consideration is that each member of the group has a conscious relation to the Self.

FIGURE 2.3

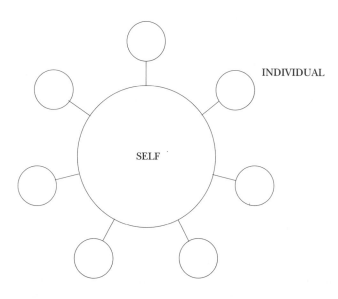

Unfortunately, this ideal situation is not the usual state of affairs. Instead, we have the following psychological arrangement (see figure 2.4). Members of a group usually do not have individual con-

FIGURE 2.4

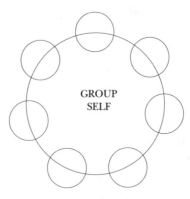

GROUP
SELF

scious relationships to the Self. Instead, the "group or corporate soul" to some extent carries the projection of the Self for some or all of the group's members. And the result is that there is a degree of *participation mystique* or collective identity. The ego is comfortable in this situation as long as it is in conformity with the general viewpoint of the group or "group spirit."

That "spirit," nevertheless, begins to reveal its "demonic" aspect whenever an individual goes against it. Then we find the very common phenomenon of the group at large ganging up on the individual who is trying to achieve, wittingly or not, a greater level of autonomy by being different. Jung has made an important statement on this subject in one of his letters as follows:

> Even a small group is ruled by a suggestive spirit which, if it is good, can have very favourable social effects, though at the expense of the mental and moral independence of the individual. The group accentuates the *ego;* one becomes braver, more presumptuous, more cocky, more insolent, more reckless; but the *Self* is diminished and gets pushed into the background in favour of the average. For this reason all weak and insecure persons belong to unions and organizations, and if possible to a nation of 80 million! Then one is a big shot, because he is identical with everybody else, but he loses his self (which is the soul the devil is after and wins!) and his individual judgment. The ego is pressed to the wall by the group only if in his judgment it

is not in accord with the group. Hence the individual in the group always tends to assent as far as possible to the majority opinion, or else to impose his opinion on the group.

The leveling influence of the group on the individual is compensated by one member of it identifying with the group spirit and becoming the Leader. As a result, prestige and power conflicts are constantly arising due to the heightened egotism of the mass man. Social egocentricity increases in proportion to the numerical strength of the group.[9]

THE SEVEN GIFTS TO THE VICTORIOUS

Under dictation, John then wrote letters to seven churches in the Roman province of Asia. In general, they start with more or less critical or threatening remarks directed to the angel of each church: "You had better shape up, or the apocalyptic Christ will get after you." Yet each letter ends with the promise of an extraordinary gift, with the proviso, "if you are victorious." For example, the apocalyptic Son of man says to Ephesus: "those who prove victorious I will feed from the tree of life set in God's paradise" (2:7). And so we need to ask ourselves first of all what it means to be "victorious." We know that John—in so far as he understood the message he was delivering—was referring to the persecution of the early Christians and to the possibility of martyrdom. Thus, to be victorious would mean concretely and literally to be true to the faith even in the face of persecution and even to the point of death. But what did this historical fact of Christian martyrdom mean psychologically? I believe it meant to have survived what Jung calls the "onslaught of instinct"—the onslaught against the ego of any affect of passionate intensity.

In this regard, there is a statement by Jung in *Symbols of Transformation* of which I am quite fond; and I have used it as an epigraph for my commentary on that work. Jung writes:

[The god] appears at first in hostile form, as an assailant with whom the hero has to wrestle. This is in keeping with the violence of all unconscious dynamism. In this manner the god manifests himself and in this form he must be overcome. The struggle has its parallel in

Jacob's wrestling with the angel at the ford Jabbok. The onslaught of instinct then becomes an experience of divinity, provided that man does not succumb to it and follow it blindly, but defends his humanity against the animal nature of the divine power.[10]

That is the dynamic I see being lived out concretely at the beginning of the Christian age. The "onslaught of instinct"—represented by the Roman Empire—was feeding upon the newly emerging Christian church; and the individuals who were able to endure that onslaught literally, even at the cost of their lives, lived out concretely the psychological scenario Jung describes. Since that confrontation of martyrdom was concrete and literal, however, the "reward" for the victorious was necessarily projected as a concrete "afterlife"— and not understood as a psychological achievement. This fact does not invalidate the historical experience, but it does de-psychologize it—while we today are obliged to withdraw as many projections as possible, including projections onto an "afterlife." The "Apocalypse," of course, has also been projected onto historical events, as well as onto a life hereafter.

Let us now consider the "gifts" themselves. (1) The church at Ephesus was promised, as we have seen, the "tree of life" in paradise. This is the same tree from which Adam and Eve were separated when expelled from the Garden of Eden; an angel with a flaming sword was set on guard to keep them from getting back to it. Yet, the commentator J.M. Ford tells us: "According to Jewish thought, paradise and the tree of life were to reappear at the end of time. . . . In the Targum of Jonathan God is said to have prepared the Garden of Eden for the righteous that they might eat of the fruit of the tree as a reward for having practiced the doctrine of the Law in this world."[11] There is another more ambiguous reference that is highly relevant. According to a mystical tradition, Rabbi Mehuniah was seated in the temple of Jerusalem in ecstasy as he described to his pupils "the secret chambers of the *merkabah*" or heavenly throne of God. His message was that only four rabbis had been able to enter the Garden of Paradise: Ben Azzai, Ben Zoma, Aher, and Akiba. "The first died, the second became insane, the third apostasized, and the fourth survived."[12] Psychologically, that is extraordinarily interesting.

(2) The church at Smyrna is told: "Even if you have to die, keep faithful, and I will give you the crown of life for your prize. . . . for those who prove victorious will come to no harm from the second death" (Rev. 2:10–11). Here the gift for the victorious is a "crown" of eternal life. This crown represents the *solificatio,* being anointed with a sun-like quality; those golden circles surrounding the head, that we often see in art, are halos of sunlight. And this imagery comes up in the dream series that Jung discusses in *Psychology and Alchemy* with additional materials to be found in *Symbols of Transformation.*[13] What is ultimately being referred to is the deification of the recipient, identifying him with the sun, just as the apocalyptic Christ is identified with the sun by virtue of his description. Now, this can be a content of psychosis and is a highly ambiguous image when encountered clinically. But, in the case of authentic individuation, it represents the "kingly" eternal quality of achieving a connection with transpersonal consciousness.

(3) To Pergamum is promised: "to those who prove victorious I will give some hidden manna and a white stone, with a new name written on it, known only to the person who receives it" (Rev. 3:17). The immediate reference here is to the sixth chapter of John's Gospel where Christ says:

> "I am the bread of life.
> Your fathers ate the manna in the desert
> and they are dead;
> but this is the bread that comes down from heaven,
> so that a man may eat it and not die.
> I am the living bread which has come down from heaven.
> Anyone who eats this bread will live for ever. . . ."
> (John 6:48–51)

This is a reference to the nourishing aspect of contact with the Self which conveys to the ego a sense of the non-temporal, the eternal dimension of existence symbolized by the idea of "eternal life."

Yet Revelation refers not just to manna but to "hidden manna," that is, to the manna contained in the ark of the Covenant hidden for safekeeping by Jeremiah in a cave on Mount Horeb at the time of the Babylonian conquest. This account can be found in 2 Maccabees (chapter 2), while the Book of Hebrews (chapter 9) confirms the tradition that the ark contained not only the tables of the Covenant but a "gold jar containing the manna" left over from the Exodus. Presumably, it is still there, yet to be found, and the victorious will receive this "hidden manna" at the End of time.[14] We see here what a rich symbolic tapestry lies behind the text, a richness that is part of the experience being described. When one has contact with the Self—the transpersonal dimension—a network of rich imagery unfolds, and meaning upon meaning reveal themselves; and one feels blessed by the network of meanings one is granted the opportunity to witness.

The victorious of Pergamum are also to be given a "white stone." That has a parallel with the alchemical *lapis,* the Philosophers' Stone, although the alchemical Philosophers' Stone is said to be red. That state of reddening, however, was achieved only after a process of going through both blackening and whitening. What we have, then, is the stone in its *albedo* aspect—yet another example of a symbol of the Self distorted somewhat, in the Book of Revelation, by local factors. The Christian dispensation—which split spirit and nature, and then identified with spirit—was in alchemical terms a vast collective *separatio, sublimatio,* and *albedo.* The "white stone," therefore, presents the *albedo* as the ultimate attainment—appropriate only for that historical stage.

(4) John is told to write to the church at Thyatira:

> "To anyone who proves victorious, and keeps working for me until the end, I will give the authority over the nations . . . to rule them with an iron scepter and shatter them like so many pots. And I will give such a person the Morning Star." (Rev. 2:26–28)

This is a direct quotation from Psalm 2, generally recognized by Jewish and Christian scholars to be a Messianic psalm. It reads in part:

> He said to me, "You are my son,
> today I have fathered you.

Ask of me, and I shall give you the nations as your birthright,
the whole wide world as your possession.
With an iron scepter you will break them,
shatter them like so many pots." (2:7–9)

Now, how are we to understand this "possession of the world" psychologically? Taken literally, of course, it just means that the divine favor will give one invincible military or political power; and there have been many times when that is how the Messianic hope was interpreted. But understood psychologically, I think these scriptures refer to the subtle yet powerful psychic effectiveness that a highly conscious individuated person has. Jung describes it in a passage in *The Undiscovered Self:*

> What does lie within our reach, however, is the change in individuals who have, or create for themselves, an opportunity to influence others of like mind. I do not mean by persuading or preaching—I am thinking, rather, of the well-known fact that anyone who has insight into his own actions, and has thus found access to the unconscious, involuntarily exercises an influence on his environment.[15]

That is a very important fact to keep in mind. If one has insight into one's own actions and has found access to the unconscious, then those psychological facts will manifest themselves; they will have some efficacy—not to serve ego purposes, you understand, since they are not under control of the ego. But, to the extent that the individual has a connection to the Self, the efficacy of the Self becomes operative in the human realm. That is how we can understand psychologically the promise of "authority over the nations."

(5) Here is what those in Sardis will receive:

> Anyone who proves victorious will be dressed, like these, in white robes; I shall not blot that name out of the book of life, but acknowledge it in the presence of my Father and his angels. (Rev. 3:5)

Again, we have a reference to the *albedo* as "white robes." This also refers to the first stage of the *coniunctio*, what is called by the alchemist Dorn the *unio mentalis*.[16] The "white robe" represents the "purification" of the ego by spiritualization which takes place in the first stage of the *coniunctio*. And at the beginning of the Christian era—when humanity was wallowing in nature and instinct—that was the highest goal that could be achieved.

The "book of life" which is mentioned here is found elsewhere, for example in Philippians 4:3 and later in Revelation 21:27. The idea is that God keeps a book listing all those who are entitled to or are destined for eternal life. One also encounters in dreams, now and then, images of a "great book," a kind of transpersonal register. It is my hypothesis that, if one reaches sufficient *consciousness of wholeness* during the ego's lifetime, then a permanent *deposit* of that consciousness will be left in the archetypal psyche—a result symbolized by the notion of being "named in the book of life." But this status requires a certain degree of individual differentiation. To the extent that one is just a mass person (just part of the contents of the pond or the collective soup) one's "name" will not be written in the "book of life." This, I caution, is a personal hypothesis for which I have not enough data to make a scientific claim.[17]

(6) And here is what the church at Philadelphia is promised by the apocalyptic Christ:

> Anyone who proves victorious I will make into a pillar in the sanctuary of my God, and it will stay there for ever; I will inscribe on it the name of my God . . . . (Rev. 3:12)

That corresponds very closely to a passage in 1 Peter, where the disciple Peter says:

> [Christ] is the living stone, rejected by human beings but chosen by God and precious to him; set yourselves close to him so that you, too, may be living stones making a spiritual house as a holy priesthood to offer the spiritual sacrifices made acceptable to God through Jesus Christ. (2:4–5)

The idea is that individuals can be "stones" that go to build up a temple. When I read of this particular gift, I thought immediately of a dream reported by Max Zeller in his book, *The Dream: The Vision of the Night,* and which the reader can find quoted in my work, *The Creation of Consciousness:*

> A temple of vast dimensions was in the process of being built. As far as I could see—ahead, behind, right and left—there were incredible numbers of people building on gigantic pillars. I, too, was building on a pillar. The whole building process was in its very beginning, but the foundation was already there, the rest of the building was starting to go up, and I and many others were working on it.[18]

When Jung was told this dream, he said: "Yes, you know, that is the temple we all build on. We don't know the people because, believe me, they build in India and China and in Russia and all over the world. That is the new religion. You know how long it will take until it is built? . . . about six hundred years."[19]

(7) Finally, the seventh church at Laodicea is promised this:

> Anyone who proves victorious I will allow to share my throne, just as I have myself overcome and have taken my seat with my Father on his throne. (Rev. 3:21)

What the apocalyptic Christ is saying in effect is this: "I will make you a king, just as I am a king." This is basically the same idea as the "crowning" we have already discussed. Concerning this question of coronation and enthronement—as it applies to psychological experience—Jung has made a particularly relevant statement. It can be found in his essay on *The Development of Personality* and also in my work, *The Christian Archetype.* In Christ's encounter with Pilate, after his arrest, Pilate was very interested in knowing if Jesus was indeed a king. After all, people had been calling him the "king of the Jews," and the Romans were understandably on the lookout for competing figures. So Pilate asked Christ, "Are you a king?" Jung once remarked: "He said, 'My kingdom is not of this world.' But 'kingdom' it was, all the same."[20] Here then is Jung's important statement:

> The story of the Temptation clearly reveals the nature of the psychic power with which Jesus came into collision: it was the power-intoxi-

cated devil of the prevailing Caesarean psychology that led him into dire temptation in the wilderness. This devil was the objective psyche that held all the peoples of the Roman Empire under its sway, and that is why it promised Jesus all the kingdoms of the earth, as if it were trying to make a Caesar of him. Obeying the inner call of his vocation, Jesus voluntarily exposed himself to the assaults of the imperialistic madness that filled everyone, conqueror and conquered alike. In this way he recognized the nature of the objective psyche which had plunged the whole world into misery and had begotten a yearning for salvation that found expression even in the pagan poets. Far from suppressing or allowing himself to be suppressed by this psychic onslaught, he let it act on him consciously, and assimilated it. Thus was world-conquering Caesarism transformed into spiritual kingship, and the Roman Empire into the universal kingdom of God that was not of this world.[21]

That passage—if the reader reflects upon it—gives us a hint of what "psychological kingship" means when it is achieved consciously. Otherwise, one falls into a state of identification with the "onslaught of instinct" and becomes, or tries to become, a literal king possessed by the power motive.

The Door, the Thief, and the Key

There are embedded in these letters to the seven churches of Asia other images of psychological significance. The Book of Revelation which contains these images is an exceedingly dense fabric of allusions. It is, moreover, of immense interest to me—and hopefully to others—to dissect this dense fabric and draw out some of the threads of reference even though we cannot consider them all. One of these is the image of "knocking at the door" which appears in Revelation 3:20 as follows:

Look, I am standing at the door, knocking. If one of you hears me calling and opens the door, I will come in to share a meal at that person's side.

This is actually a common dream image, to find someone "knocking at the door"—although sometimes this dream person is doing a little more than knocking, is pushing in the door or the window and is decidedly more importunate. This is an indication that the unconscious is clamoring for admission to consciousness; and it is important to follow the proper internal procedure as opposed to the proper external procedure. If strangers come to one's door literally and clamor for admission, it is not advisable to be quick in admitting them. Quite different rules prevail, however, in the inner life. This is an important principle since we observe again and again that the dream ego behaves towards the inner circumstance the way it would in the outer circumstance. Eventually, if enough wisdom has been brought to the issue at the conscious level, the dream ego will recognize on the spot: "Oh, this belongs to the other category of experience, and I am supposed to open the door and show immediate hospitality, even though it is a stranger."[22]

Another important image appears in Revelation 3:3, where the apocalyptic Christ says to one of the churches:

> Repent! If you do not wake up, I shall come to you like a thief, and you will have no idea at what hour I shall come upon you.

This theme appears elsewhere, for instance Luke 12:35–40:

> "See that you have your belts done up and your lamps lit. Be like people waiting for their master to return from the wedding feast, ready to open the door as soon as he comes and knocks. Blessed those servants whom the master finds awake when he comes. In truth I tell you, he will do up his belt, sit them down at table and wait on them. . . . You may be quite sure of this, that if the householder had known at what time the burglar would come, he would not have let anyone break through the wall of his house. You too must stand ready, because the Son of man is coming at an hour you do not expect."

Consider also 1 Thessalonians:

> About times and dates, brothers, there is no need to write to you for you are well aware in any case that the Day of the Lord is going to

come like a thief in the night. It is when people are saying, "How quiet and peaceful it is" that sudden destruction falls on them, as suddenly as labour pains come on a pregnant woman; and there is no escape. (5:1-3)

This imagery of the apocalyptic Christ as a forceful "burglar" becomes applicable if one has not paid attention to an earlier gentler "knocking." The response from the unconscious gets more importunate and forces its way in violently; sometimes it does that by creating literal accidents—when one's attention is forcibly removed from external habitual concern. Then, one is *forcibly* shifted to another level.

Consider now the image of the "key" in Revelation 3:7 where the apocalyptic Christ is speaking of himself:

> "Here is the message of the holy and true one who has the key of David, so that when he opens, no one will close, and when he closes, no one will open" (see figure 2.5).

This is a direct quotation from Isaiah where Yahweh is talking to Shebna at the time that Babylon is besieging Jerusalem. Thus, that event is occurring at an apocalyptic moment in the history of Israel. Yahweh tells Shebna, who is the current master of the palace, that he is fed up with Shebna's grandiose ways, his putting on airs, and he is going to depose him of his job and give it to somebody else:

> I shall summon my servant
> Eliakim son of Hilkiah.
> I shall dress him in your tunic,
> I shall put your sash round his waist,
> I shall invest him with your authority;
> and he will be a father
> to the inhabitants of Jerusalem
> and to the House of Judah.
> I shall place the key of David's palace
> on his shoulder;
> when he opens, no one will close,
> when he closes, no one will open. (22:20–22)

FIGURE 2.5

The Key of David and the Open Door. from *The Douce Apocalypse.* 13th century, C.E. Illumination. Bodleian Library, Oxford.

Now, why make so much of this image of the "key"? It is because the grand eschatological event in the Book of Revelation can be connected to a concrete, specific, historical event involving specific persons. The connection of the general to the specific demonstrates that different levels of the psyche are interwoven into the text of this scripture in the same way that happens in dreams.

When one works on a dream of any magnitude, one finds the same phenomenon of various components. Some aspects of the dream derive perhaps from yesterday; other aspects derive from one's personal childhood; while some aspects may derive from the archetypal level with historical antecedents that have parallels hundreds of years ago. And those threads will all be woven together into the fabric of the dream. Which threads you recognize will depend on your level of consciousness and what particular theories of the psyche you hold to begin with. But the dream interpreter will *not* be able to see any more than his or her "school" of psychology permits. That is why it is so important for Analytical psychologists to study mythology and the various manifestations of archetypal imagery: unless one is fairly acquainted with these materials, one will not be able to recognize the profounder threads in spontaneous dreamwork.

There are other important biblical references to the "key." In Revelation 1:18, the apocalyptic Christ says, "I hold the keys of death and of Hades." In 9:1, an angel is given the key to the shaft leading down to the abyss. In Matthew, Christ says to Peter: "You are Peter and on this rock I will build my community. And the gates of the underworld can never overpower it. I will give you the keys of the kingdom of Heaven: whatever you bind on earth will be bound in heaven; whatever you loose on earth will be loosed in heaven" (16:18–19). That particular passage is the basis for the Roman Catholic Church's claim to authority; the Pope's seal has depicted upon it the crossed keys of these "keys of the Kingdom."

All of these data mean that we have four different kinds of keys: 1) the concrete, literal, historical key to the palace of David; 2) the more symbolical keys of death and the underworld; 3) the key to the abyss; 4) and keys to the Kingdom of Heaven. Psychologically, one should understand that this variety of descriptions refers to different aspects of the same "key"—which basically represents that living entity, that symbolic, operative efficacy that "opens" the unconscious. The unconscious may be opened in its heavenly form, it may be opened in a hellish form, or it may be opened in the way one relates to a concrete situation as represented by the key to the palace of David. The image of the key exhibits a variety of aspects.

THE RAPTURE

The image of the "rapture" (included in my chart of the "Apocalypse archetype," figure 1.1) is introduced scripturally by Revelation 3.10:

"Because you have kept my commandment to persevere, I will keep you safe in the time of trial which is coming for the whole world, to put the people of the world to the test."

This text is usually taken by fundamentalist scholars to refer to the sparing of believing Christians at the time of the great tribulation and the coming of the apocalyptic Christ. The just ones are to be seized, removed from earth, and deposited safely in heaven. One so-called "proof text" is John 14:2 where we read: "In my Father's house there are many places to live in; otherwise I would have told you. I am going now to prepare a place for you." The chief "rapture" text, however, is 1 Thessalonians 4:16-17:

At the signal given by the voice of the Archangel and the trumpet of God, the Lord himself will come down from heaven; those who have died in Christ will be the first to rise, and only after that shall we who remain alive be taken up in the clouds, together with them to meet the Lord in the air. This is the way we shall be with the Lord for ever.

If one watches certain television evangelists, it is clear that this image is taken literally by many people—one can even send away for a painting of the "rapture" with empty cars littering the freeways of Los Angeles since believing Christians have been "caught up" in the air! It is a serious and widespread conviction. Fifty to sixty percent of the American population believe in the literal interpretation of the Bible while the idea of the "rapture" is very widespread among mainstream fundamentalist churches. This belief allows people to anticipate the very real terrors of the Apocalypse with relative equanimity since they are sure to be "caught up" and spared.

A more negative interpretation is justified, however, for those who joyfully expect literal rescue from the coming tribulation on the basis of their elect status. Such a state of mind is a dehumanizing inflation that seeks permanent release from egohood and materiality. To embrace such a literal eschatological fantasy means, in effect, that the individual has already been "raptured" (literally "seized"). These people, therefore, have abandoned allegiance to the human enterprise and abdicated commitment to the historical process.[23]

Those of us who are more psychologically alert cannot take this imagery literally, but must admit that it is part of the "living myth" and deserves to be understood. I think the "rapture" refers to the capacity to bear or endure great hardship and distress: provided one understands the circumstances to be meaningful, provided one sees the events one is suffering to be part of a larger purposeful pattern with a goal. That gives the sufferer a certain viewpoint "above" the difficult circumstances, so to speak, and outside the immediate concrete events. It does not put one in heavenly bliss, to be sure, but it does make the events bearable. Psychological experience bears out that way of thinking; it is, at any rate, a way to understand the "rapture" as a symbol.

3 Revelation: Chapters 4, 5

HEAVENLY KINGSHIP

Chapter 4 of Revelation continues the grand vision of the numinosum with the image of God as a great king, "One who was sitting on the throne." This image is operative throughout the Old Testament, of course, where God was thought of as king of the world; it is illustrated well by Psalm 47:

Clap your hands, all peoples,
acclaim God with shouts of joy.

For Yahweh, the Most High, is glorious,
the great king over all the earth.
He brings peoples under our yoke
and nations under our feet.

He chooses for us our birthright,
the pride of Jacob whom he loves.

God goes up to shouts of acclaim,
Yahweh to a fanfare on the ram's horn.

Let the music sound for our God, let it sound,
let the music sound for our king, let it sound.

For he is king of the whole world;
learn the music, let it sound for God!

God reigns over the nations,
seated on his holy throne.

The leaders of the nations rally
to the people of the God of Abraham.
The shields of the earth belong to God,
who is exalted on high.

This image of God as "universal king" is central to the Apocalypse
archetype. It has a prominent place in the chart above (see figure
1.1) and is related to the technical term "Messiah." Messiah means
"anointed" in Hebrew; the word "Christ" is the equivalent Greek
term for the "anointed" one. Thus, the king in the Bible is one who
has received his royal status by way of a sacred anointing.[1]

We have already discussed Christ's claim of "kingship" at the
questioning of Pilate and have called attention to Jung's remark
that a kingdom "not of this world" is a kingdom nonetheless. The
point is that the concrete king represents the divine on earth,
while—psychologically—the image of the "king" represents the
Self. Indeed, it is from the Self that the "divine right" of kings
comes. There is much psychological insight to be gained by the
study of the origin and evolution of kingship in early societies; and
John Perry's work, *Lord of the Four Quarters,* is a very good treatment
of this subject. The author has assembled mythological materials
concerning kingship from all over the world, demonstrating how
human government evolved out of the phenomenon of sacred kingship in which the king was quite literally the god.[2] "King," therefore,
represents the ultimate authority—in fact, "authority" is a term
most applicable to this image.

This brings up a basic question in the course of progressive self-
understanding: What is one's authority? By what particular authority, ultimately, does one live one's life; by whom or by what is one
commanded? I do not think this question is asked in depth very
often, even though it is crucial. When I state that the image of the
"king" is a symbol of the Self, that means one's *ultimate* authority
(if one reaches conscious awareness of it) is internal. And to the
extent that this is consciously realized, one achieves a stand-

point—a true counterpole which can stand over and against the world. If we put the world on one side of a scales and the individual in relation to the Self on the other side, they balance. And this balance is a requirement of consciousness. It is part of the psychological symbolism that lies behind the drama of Christ's being challenged by the worldly Pilate. Christ could identify himself as a "king not of this world" because that is individuation symbolism, relevant to everyone who strikes deeply enough. It means that any person who has a conscious relation to the Self is in a certain sense a "king." Yet one has to say in the same breath that it also means to be a "servant"—because ultimately it is not the ego that is the king.

This vision in chapter 4 is actually a mandala: the divine throne in the center, the outer circle of twenty-four elders on their thrones, the four animal-like entities, the seven lights, and a surrounding sea of glass.

THE SEA OF GLASS

This "sea of glass" is sometimes referred to as a "sea of crystal," but the important Greek term here is *hyalos* which literally means "glass," pointing us to the symbolism of glass. John tells us in the Jerusalem Bible version that "Between the throne and myself was a sea that seemed to be made of glass, like crystal" (Jerusalem Bible, Rev. 4:6). As I have already mentioned, the "heavenly court" to which the visionary has been called is the divine prototype of the earthly tabernacle; what John sees above corresponds to the furniture that existed in the tabernacle or temple down below. And this is true even of the "sea of glass." Outside the temple at Jerusalem was a great basin fifteen feet in diameter and seven and one-half feet deep. It was called the "Sea" or a "Bronze Sea" and was used for ritual washings (see figure 5.1). The Gnostics, however, provide an interesting variation on its use. According to the Apocryphon of John found in the Nag Hammadi Library, the divine Monad is a "monarchy" (someone sitting on a throne) surrounded by a sea of "light-water":

> For it is he who looks at himself in his light which surrounds him,
> namely the spring of the water of life. And it is he who gives to all the
> aeons and in every way, and who gazes upon his image which he sees
> in the spring of the Spirit. It is he who puts his desire in his water-light
> which is in the spring of the pure light-water which surrounds him.3

God contemplates his own image reflected in this heavenly sea
before his throne; and there is a hint that this heavenly sea is also
an agency for some later emanations—since his "reflection" was
transmitted thereby into more distant areas.

I have discussed the symbolism of "glass" elsewhere, because the
history of glass and its imagery is very significant psychologically.4
Glass was discovered in Egypt probably in the sixteenth century
B.C.E.; and the Egyptians subsequently became highly proficient in
glassmaking. But, interestingly enough, glass is mentioned only
once in the Hebrew Bible where Job says of Wisdom, "Neither gold
nor glass compares with her" (Job 28:17). In other words, glass
could have a very high value in the Ancient Near East; but it was not
used much by the Israelites themselves perhaps, as scholars sometimes suggest, due to their antipathy toward Egyptian products. I
suggest this antipathy is also toward Greek rationalism because
"glass" represents that kind of consciousness. The Greeks' word for
glass *(hyalos)*—which may have an Egyptian etymology—has given us
"hyaline," meaning glassy; the medical term, hyaline cartilage,
refers to a glassy transparent kind of cartilage. It is a striking feature
of glass that it is transparent, that we can see through it even though
it has a permanent, indestructible quality. It can be broken, of
course, but it is not biodegradable and endures indefinitely. That is
one reason why the "vitreous body" was a synonym for the indestructible Philosophers' Stone of alchemy; *vitrum* is the Latin word
for "glass." Glass associates to bottles, windows, eyeglasses, mirrors,
microscopes, telescopes—all these things that promote the ability to
see. Thus, I consider our literal glass to be the earthly (ego) equivalent of the heavenly (archetypal) sea of glass before Yahweh's
throne.

All of this is relevant to dream interpretation because glass is not
an uncommon feature in dreams, often as vessels but sometimes as

windows or other devices for seeing. I generally consider this imagery to refer to a person's current rational consciousness that contains his or her world view. If the dream depicts the "breaking of glass," that indicates a shattering of a particular level of consciousness—hopefully in preparation for an enlargement. Smaller world views have to be broken through in order to make room for the larger. In a "nuclear bomb" dream which we will examine below, the dreamer walks out upon the devastated landscape to find a lot of "broken glass," which we can say is a symbolic feature of our age. One of the authentic prophets of our time, the poet T.S. Eliot, wrote in *The Hollow Men* of "rats' feet over broken glass/In our dry cellar" as a sign of the times.[5]

THE FOUR ANIMALS OR LIVING CREATURES

We need now to consider John's vision of what the Jerusalem Bible calls the "four animals" and the New Jerusalem version calls "living creatures" located around the divine throne. John writes:

> In the middle of the throne and around it, were four living creatures all studded with eyes, in front and behind. The first living creature was like a lion, the second like a bull, the third living creature had a human face, and the fourth living creature was like a flying eagle. Each of the four living creatures had six wings and was studded with eyes all the way round as well as inside; and day and night they never stopped singing . . . . (Rev. 4:6–8)

This imagery is a variation or a simplification of Ezekiel's vision which I have taken up in *The Mysterium Lectures* and other writings.[6] Ezekiel says in his first chapter that each of the four animals had four different faces; but here, the four faces are distributed among the four figures. In either case, we have a divine quaternity since these animals surround the throne; yet the quaternity is three-quarters theriomorphic and only one-quarter human. That indicates the degree of humanization of the God-image that had been achieved at the time of the image's appearance. By contrast, today—in the most highly developed of modern individuals, as demonstrated by depth analysis—we find images of the God with fully three-quarters of the image humanized. There is, therefore, such a thing as psychological progress, even though the collective does not demonstrate that potential very clearly. In this regard, we must not be too optimistic.

THE APOCALYPTIC LAMB

Then we are told about the "Lamb." Revelation 5:1–7 reads as follows:

> I saw that in the right hand of the One sitting on the throne there was a scroll that was written on back and front and was sealed with seven seals. Then I saw a powerful angel who called with a loud voice, "Who is worthy to open the scroll and break its seals?" But there was no one, in heaven or on the earth or under the earth, who was able to open the scroll and read it. I wept bitterly because nobody could be found to open the scroll and read it, but one of the elders said to me, "Do not weep. Look, the Lion of the tribe of Judah, the Root of David, has triumphed, and so he will open the scroll and its seven seals."
>
> Then I saw, in the middle of the throne with its four living creatures animals and the circle of the elders, a Lamb standing that seemed to have been sacrificed; it had seven horns, and it had seven eyes, which are the seven Spirits that God has sent out over the whole world. The Lamb came forward to take the scroll from the right hand of the One sitting on the throne . . . .

How are we to understand this Lamb? The Greek word is *arnion*, which can be translated either as "lamb" or "ram"—and it does matter which way one translates, for different sets of association follow. When John the Baptist first saw Jesus in the Gospel of John, he exclaimed, "Look, there is the lamb of God that takes away the sin of the world" (1:29). During the Exodus, on the night of the Passover, the blood of the sacrificial lamb protected the Israelites from the avenging angel. On the other hand, when Abraham was spared the sacrifice of his son Isaac, he found a ram caught in a thicket that was to provide the sacrificial substitute. And I think it is relevant that Aries or the "Ram" was the spring sign of the zodiac which was ending at the time of Christ, who represents the first "fish" in the subsequent sign of Pisces. This means that in the image of the ram we are dealing with an "apocalyptic moment" of transition from one aeon to another.[7]

The ram, in its behavior and its symbolism, is a rather fiery, aggressive animal; the lamb, on the other hand, is associated with innocence and the sacrificial state. But there is no doubt that the apocalyptic Lamb in the Book of Revelation behaves every bit as much ram as lamb; as Jung says, "Altogether it must have looked pretty awful" (see figure 3.1).[8] It had seven horns and seven eyes, and we are told specifically that the seven eyes are the seven Spirits of Yahweh that roam about the earth. This indicates that the sevenfold nature of the deity has been consolidated in the image of the Lamb, the horns corresponding to various divine potencies. Jung tells us furthermore in *Mysterium Coniunctionis* that theriomorphic symbolism indicates the transconscious nature of the psychic content:

> The elevation of the human figure to a king or divinity, and on the other hand its representation in subhuman, theriomorphic form, are indications of the *transconscious character* of the pairs of opposites . . . . The pairs of opposites constitute the phenomenology of the paradoxical *[S]elf*, man's totality.[9]

In our text, these opposites are alluded to in a subtle way by the word *arnion* (which can mean ram or lamb) but more explicitly by the persistent imagery of lion and lamb. We are told that the "Lion of the tribe of Judah" has triumphed, yet we are immediately presented with a Lamb: the lion and the lamb are certainly opposites. The "Lion of Judah," incidentally, is a Messianic title which goes back to Genesis 49:9.[10] The lion and the lamb—as antitheses—represent the double nature of this apocalyptic king or Messiah, as Jung discusses in *Aion*.[11] But the psychological point is that when we encounter a manifestation of the Self, the opposites are a prominent part of its phenomenology. And the lion and the lamb—the ram and the lamb—are examples of that phenomenon.

FIGURE 3.1

Artist unknown. *Lamb of God.* 11–12th century, C.E. Detail from the apse fresco in the church of St. Climent in Taüll.

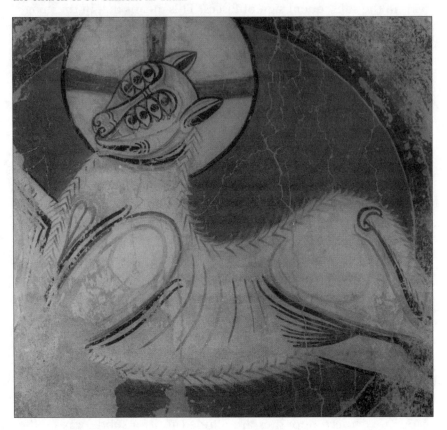

THE EYE OF GOD

We have been told that the apocalyptic Lamb had seven eyes, which are the seven eyes of God. This image of the "eye of God" is very important as I discuss at some length elsewhere; and it is crucial to the Apocalypse archetype.[12] The coming of the Self into visibility is accompanied by the ego's experience of being looked at, being stripped of all disguises and seen for *exactly what one is.* That is no easy experience to endure. It has the nature of the so-called "Final

Judgment," which is no fabrication of priests imposed on human beings from the outside; it is, in fact, an archetypal psychic reality projected from the unconscious into mythological material. Practically all the religions of the world have the notion of a Final Judgment—not necessarily coming in some future time, as in the Book of Revelation, but coming just after death. This objective judgment (so often projected into the afterlife) is nevertheless an experience one does not need to die to have.

In his collection of apocalyptic dreams, *Dreaming the End of the World,* Michael Ortiz Hill records the dream of a Dr. Michihiko Hachiya. It might be noted that this author is not an analyst nor is his approach primarily a psychological one (his generalizations have a quasi-Buddhist quality), but he is very clearly gripped by the Apocalypse archetype and has an earnest concern about the coming catastrophe. While Hill tells us virtually nothing about the personal reality of the dreamers—so essential for understanding—in this case we learn that a Japanese man dreamed the following on August 24th, 1945, about three weeks after experiencing the nuclear bombing of Hiroshima:

> [It seems] I was in Tokyo after the great earthquake and around me were decomposing bodies heaped in piles, all of whom were looking right at me. I saw an eye sitting in the palm of a girl's hand. Suddenly it turned and leaped into the sky and then came flying back toward me, so that looking up I could see a great bare eyeball, bigger than life hovering over my head, staring point-blank at me. I was powerless to move. I awakened short of breath and my heart pounding.[13]

Look at what has happened here: A man has had the shattering experience of actually witnessing a nuclear bomb explosion, an experience activating the Apocalypse archetype within his psyche— which in turn expresses itself as the "eye of the Other" scrutinizing the dreamer. There is nothing about being victim of a nuclear bomb in itself that leads to the idea of being looked at with a great bare eyeball: that image comes from the psyche. It is the psyche's response to this terrible experience. In yet another dream, a great fireball is described; and the dreamer reports: "The fireball is fixed, yet moving, staring at me like an eye" (see figure 3.2).[14]

FIGURE 3.2

Jan Provost (1465–1529). *Allegory*. 16th century, C.E. Louvre, Paris.

THE POWER OF SACRIFICE

The Book of Revelation has more to say about the Lamb:

> The Lamb came forward to take the scroll from the right hand of the
> One sitting on the throne, and when he took it, the four living crea-
> tures prostrated themselves before him and with them the twenty-four
> elders; each one of them was holding a harp and had a golden bowl full
> of incense which are the prayers of the saints. They sang a new hymn:
>
> > You are worthy to take the scroll
> > and break its seals,
> > because you were sacrificed, and with your blood
> > you bought people for God
> > of every race, language, people and nation
> > and made them a line of kings and priests for God,
> > to rule the world.
>
> In my vision, I heard the sound of an immense number . . . loudly
> chanting:
>
> > Worthy is the Lamb that was sacrificed
> > to receive power, riches, wisdom,
> > strength, honour, glory and blessing. (5:7-12)

This passage is indicating that sacrifice can generate huge
power; because it is specifically "power" and "glory" that is imputed
to the Lamb from the fact that it was sacrificed. It bought its power
with its sacrificial blood. And that brings up the complex question
of how we are to understand "sacrifice" psychologically.

Fortunately, we have a splendid discussion of this subject by
Jung. It can be found in his essay on *Transformation Symbolism in the
Mass,* specifically in the section, "The Psychological Meaning of
Sacrifice."[15] Here, Jung goes into full, concrete, personal detail—a
style for which he is not known in his later work. He discusses what
it means for an individual to sacrifice, for that person to give up
something of value, to offer it as a gift; and he says such gifts always
carry a "personal claim" with them. Let us remind ourselves of that:

no one, not even a particularly generous person, can escape the
nature of the psyche which places a claim on every gift, what Jung
calls the "implied intention of receiving something in return."[16]
The only question is whether or not one is conscious of the claim.
That makes all the difference: If we are conscious of our claim, then
we can sacrifice it—for it is in our possession to begin with. But if a
person is not conscious of the *intent* to receive something in return,
it has not been owned and cannot be given up. Jung writes:

> What I sacrifice is my own selfish claim, and by doing this I give up
> myself. Every sacrifice is therefore, to a greater or lesser degree, a self-
> sacrifice. The degree to which it is so depends on the significance of
> the gift. If it is of great value to me and touches my most personal feel-
> ings, I can be sure that in giving up my egoistic claim I shall challenge
> my ego personality to revolt. I can also be sure that the power which
> suppresses this claim, and thus suppresses me, must be the self. Hence
> it is the self that causes me to make the sacrifice; nay more, it compels
> me to make it. The self is the sacrificer, and I am the sacrificed gift, the
> human sacrifice.[17]

Jung considers the classic situation of Abraham who was commanded to sacrifice his own son, and then continues:

> Now, since the relation of the ego to the Self is like that of the son to
> the father, we can say that when the Self calls on us to sacrifice our-
> selves, it is really carrying out the sacrificial act on itself. . . . We have
> seen that a sacrifice only takes place when we feel the Self actually car-
> rying it out on ourselves. We may also venture to surmise that in so far
> as the Self stands to us in the relation of father to son, the Self in some
> sort feels our sacrifice as a sacrifice of itself. From that sacrifice we gain
> ourselves—our "self"—for we have only what we give. But what does
> the Self gain? We see it entering into manifestation, freeing itself from
> unconscious projection, and, as it grips us, entering into our lives and
> so passing from unconsciousness into consciousness, from potentiality
> into actuality. . . . in becoming ourself it has become man.[18]

Sacrifice, then, is a process that corresponds to the incarnation
myth. It is a process that explains why the sacrificed Lamb has so
much power (see figure 3.3).

FIGURE 3.3

William Blake. *And my Servant Job shall pray for you,* from *Illustrations of the Book of Job.* 1826, Engraving.

The archetype of "Sacrifice," of course, can also express itself in psycho-pathological form; it can be perverted. The so-called martyr complexes are an example of that. And it is not uncommon to see someone (quite often a woman) who presents herself as the "suffering one" but with an "iron fist" just below the surface—with a claim that is totally unconscious to that person but obvious to everyone else. Or there are cases where the living out of the martyr role has the effect not so much as a power motive against one's environment but—more inwardly—against one's own developmental urge. Then the perversion of true sacrifice becomes a means of arresting one's own psychological development and keeping one from confronting ongoing life.

With regard to this issue of arrested development, let us note that it is sometimes a matter of having ignored in one's self the inferior function—projecting it instead upon a spouse or a child. And when that child leaves home to live its own life or the spouse dies or there is a divorce, the experience may be so catastrophic that images of the Apocalypse archetype appear in one's dreams. This is due to the fact that when one encounters voluntarily or is forced by difficult circumstances to encounter the fourth and final function—the one that "nature has worked on but a little"—it drags up with it the whole collective unconscious. The primitive state of that function carries the power of the primitive Self: and it is no longer adequate to describe the experience in terms of typology, because the typological schema has been transcended by the much larger theme of "revelation." That is, of course, the meaning of "apocalypse" with all its ambiguous features.

4 Revelation: Chapters 6, 7

THE NUMBER SEVEN

From this great sea of imagery which can so easily inundate us, I would like now to take up the symbolism of the number "seven." Revelation has already introduced us to a book (a "scroll" in the translation) that has seven seals or fastenings on it; and they are to be opened one by one. Here, then, is the image of seven. But we have already encountered it in earlier chapters: seven lamps before the throne of God, seven stars in the hand of the apocalyptic Christ, seven angels, seven churches; seven horns and seven eyes on the Lamb; and now these seven seals on the scroll—the seventh of which, as we shall learn, leads to seven trumpets. The number "seven" is being shouted at us! Indeed, one could say that the whole Book of Revelation is a bombardment with the archetype of "Seven"—going on and on, endlessly.[1] It deserves our considered attention.

Yet it is difficult for the modern mind to appreciate the way that the ancients thought of numbers. Jung tells us that "Numbers" are archetypes; and as one makes some connection with the unconscious, one does begin to sense the numinosity that accompanies certain numbers. The ancients were not so remote from the origin of numbers as we are; and so they had more of a sense of that numinosity, a feeling for what we now call their qualitative aspect as opposed to their quantitative aspect. This qualitative aspect of numbers has been almost totally lost today but was familiar still to the Jewish philosopher Philo Judaeus (first century C.E.) who wrote an encomium of the number seven. As an example of the modern mind's reaction to the archetype, on the other hand, Nahum Glatzer edits out of his work, *The Essential Philo,* an extensive excursus on "seven"—evidently considering it too picturesque or bizarre to be relevant and not worthy of our homage.[2]

Philo wrote an essay on the Creation—itself a commentary on Genesis—where he speaks of the six days of God's creative acts followed by the very significant seventh day of rest. He says:

> Now when the whole world had been brought to completion in accordance with the properties of six, a perfect number, the Father invested with dignity the seventh day which comes next, extolling it and pronouncing it holy; for it is the festival, not of a single city or country, but of the universe, and it alone strictly deserves to be called "public" as belonging to all people and the birthday of the world. I doubt whether anyone could adequately celebrate the properties of the number 7, for they are beyond all words. Yet the fact that it is more wondrous than all that is said about it is no reason for maintaining silence regarding it.

Indeed, Philo proceeds to talk about this wondrous ineffable "seven" for about twenty pages or so. In part, he says:

> 7 (or "7th") exhibits yet another beauty belonging to it, a most sacred object for our mind to ponder. Being made up as it is of 3 and 4 it is a presentation of all that is naturally steadfast and upright in the universe. How it is this, we must point out. The right-angled triangle, the starting point of figures of a definite shape, is made up of certain numbers, namely 3 and 4 and 5: 3 and 4, the constituent parts of 7, produce the right angle . . . . Now if the right-angled triangle is the starting-point of figures of a definite kind, and the essential factor in this triangle, namely the right angle, is supplied by the numbers which constitute 7, namely 3 and 4 together, 7 would reasonably be regarded as the fountain-head of every figure and every definite shape. . . . So august is the dignity inherent by nature in the number 7, that it has a unique relation distinguishing it from all other numbers within the decade. . . . It is the nature of 7 alone, as I have said, neither to beget nor to be begotten.[3]

In the discussion of the triangle's properties here, the reader may recognize the Pythagorean Theorem of geometry. Philo is also saying that seven is a prime number, that it has no factors or is not a multiple of some number (in this scheme, one is not a real number). Therefore, seven is not "begotten." But it is also true that seven "does not beget," since within the series of ten (the "decade") there is no room for it to beget; a multiple of seven (such as seven times two) would go beyond the series of ten. While we observe in Philo's discussion how fascinated the ancients were with the properties of prime numbers, we are also able to witness the way that the ancient mind was still in touch with living symbolism and could think of numbers as being "begotten" or "begetting."[4]

We must now ask ourselves what it means to be assaulted by the number "seven," as we are in the Book of Revelation. Let us recall important items where this number comes up in our culture generally. There are the seven days of Creation; the seven days of the week and seven basic metals of alchemy, both of which are derived from the seven planets of the Ptolemaic system; Shakespeare informs us that there are seven ages or stages of life, a notion going all the way back to the Athenian lawgiver Solon (sixth century B.C.E.); and there are the seven wonders of the world; seven deadly sins; seven gifts of the Holy Spirit—and the list goes on. But, among these, the most important reference is to the seven planets of antiquity which were thought of as a planetary "ladder."[5] The ascending soul had to ascend the seven steps of this planetary ladder in order to reach the eighth step—which was the sphere of the fixed stars and, therefore, the Eternal. In *Psychology and Alchemy*, Jung presents a few dreams in the series he is discussing that involve the number seven. In the dream that follows one with the image of "many ladders," "The father calls out anxiously, 'That is the seventh!'."[6] Why should the father be so anxious? The answer is that this number fits the imagery of the Apocalypse—about which it is appropriate to be anxious. The connection of the planetary ladder with initiation symbolism world-wide indicates that one of the basic meanings of the number "seven" is that it symbolizes the process of psychological transformation: movement through a series of stages as part of an initiation process.

"Seven," then, is not just an integer but an image of development. For instance, in Proverbs we read: "For though the upright falls seven times, he gets up again; the wicked are the ones who stumble in adversity" (24:16). This illustrates the point that the number seven is a transformational image. Furthermore, as Philo points out, seven is meaningfully the sum of three and four. I have discussed this symbolism of "three and four" in the chapter, "The Trinity Archetype and the Dialectic of Development," in my *Ego and Archetype* and consider there the symbolism of the number "three" to refer very often to egohood.[7] This is because the number refers to processes in time and space that go through a three-fold sequence (for example: past, present, and future; beginning, middle, and end). On the other hand, "four" is the number of wholeness beyond space and time (which are, by the way, categories of consciousness) and thus tends to represent static "Eternity."

If we apply these considerations to the relationship between the numbers three and four, they can also apply—as Jung points out—to the relationship between the numbers seven and eight. Seven is next to the image of eight as a "totality"; yet seven, like three, is a sequence of stages or a "ladder" in a life process. To oversimplify—in order that these matters might stick in the mind—I suggest that "three" refers to a process of an *ego-based* operation that has the possibility of leading to the experience of the Self from the standpoint of the ego. On the other hand, "seven" refers to a process of a *Self-based* dynamic sequence, leading to an experience of the Self from the standpoint of the Self. As I have indicated earlier, the basic theme of the apocalyptic process is the coming of the Self into conscious realization which characteristically brings with it a good bit of anxiety. We can understand the dream that says anxiously that the "seventh" is on its way, if we realize that the number "seven" is the process whereby the Self comes into realization through its own terms.

One final item in this section for the reader to ponder is the alchemical "hidden magical Septenary"—for which I merely provide the diagram from Jung's *Mysterium Coniunctionis* (see figure 4.1). The "little inner circle" corresponds for Jung to the Mercurial Fountain in the *Rosarium* pictures of his essay, "The Psychology of

FIGURE 4.1

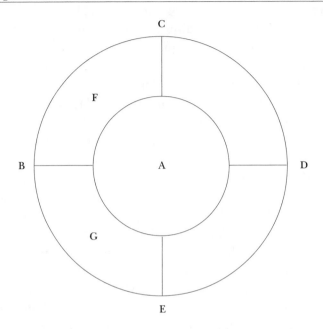

the Transference."⁸ The letters A through G (taken as a whole) form a seven-fold mandala of completeness.

The Four Horsemen

Let us return now to the text of Revelation and the beginning of chapter six:

> Then, in my vision, I saw the Lamb break one of the seven seals, and I heard one of the four living creatures shout in a voice like thunder, "Come!" Immediately I saw a white horse appear, and its rider was holding a bow; he was given a victor's crown and he went away, to go from victory to victory. (6:1–2)

Then a second seal was broken; and there came another horse, this one "bright red." And its rider was told "to take away peace from the earth and set people killing each other; and he was given a huge sword" (6:3–4). The Lamb broke a third seal as a "black" horse appeared with the rider holding a pair of scales. We hear a voice shouting: "A day's wages for a quart of corn, and a day's wages for three quarts of barley" (6:6). When the fourth seal was broken, a "deathly pale" horse arrived: and "its rider was called Death [the Jerusalem Bible translates "Plague"] and Hades followed at his heels" (6:8) (see figure 4.2).

Observe what is happening here. I have been discussing an assault by the septenary, yet out of this seven-sealed book comes an assault by the quaternity—in the form of four horsemen. It is a double assault; the assault of the quaternity is hidden in the assault of the septenary. There is, moreover, a parallel to this passage in the sixth chapter of Zechariah where the prophet says: "Again I raised my eyes, and this is what I saw: four chariots coming out between two mountains . . . . The first chariot had red horses, the second chariot had black horses, the third chariot had white horses and the fourth chariot had vigorous, piebald horses" (1–4). They are identified by an angel as the "four winds of heaven" and are told to "patrol the world." And both scriptures present us with a color sequence which is also characteristic of alchemy. In alchemy, the sequence is typically three-fold: in the order black*(nigredo),* white *(albedo),* and red *(rubedo);* although sometimes there is a fourth "yellowing" or gold color *(citrinitas).* If we assume the alchemical sequence to be the natural order, then Revelation has reversed the red and the black, perhaps referring to the generally negative appraisal that all things "red" were receiving about this time in religious history.

What is more important, however, is the problem here of "three plus one." It appears in Revelation as three straight-forward colors, and then a "pale" one. The word in Greek is *kloros* and actually means "green" (from it we get "chlorophyll"); but this was also the accepted color of cadavers, and from that the meaning of "paleness" derives. In Zechariah also three straight-forward colors are followed by a more ambiguous "spotted" fourth. Jung has familiarized us with this issue (corresponding to the alchemical "Axiom of Maria") and which we now understand refers to the three functions

FIGURE 4.2

Albrecht Dürer (1471–1528). *Four Horsemen of the Apocalypse.* ca.1498. Woodcut.

of consciousness—plus the fourth, which is so very troublesome.[9] The colors as well as the functions of the four horsemen of the Apocalypse, who are going to wreak havoc on the world, make the same point. The second, third, and fourth horsemen are clearly of the same sort: each dispensing calamity—people killing each other, famine, and plague. But the first horseman's role is not clearly negative; indeed, associations to his white horse are usually quite positive. In the nineteenth chapter of the Book of Revelation, the apocalyptic Christ is riding a white horse.

It is very interesting to observe what various commentators through the ages have done with this material—which has been around for so long that countless psyches have had a chance to reflect on it and bring to it their own fantasies. Such attention yields interesting and significant auxiliary material when one is considering what this imagery means psychologically. There are three main opinions with regard to this first rider on a white horse. Some have decided that the figure on the white horse is, in fact, the same as the figure described later as Christ—the apocalyptic Christ himself joining these other plagues. A second view is that the horseman is merely imitating the apocalyptic Christ and is, instead, the Anti-Christ who rides a white horse to deceive people. The third major interpretation is that he is just another avenging angel like the others, representing some kind of war or domination.[10] And there are other views, of course, including that of the scholar Gilles Quispel who takes what we have already referred to as the "preterist" view—understanding the symbols of Revelation to refer to historical events that had just happened. Thus, for him, all four horsemen of the Apocalypse refer to the Parthians who were waiting on the border to attack the Roman Empire. In any event, the basic point is that we have three horsemen whose function is rather clear—and a fourth whose function is sufficiently ambiguous for it to lead to a lot of disagreement. Any analyst who is alert to the symbolism of the "three plus one" will find it in patient material very frequently.

THE VENGEANCE OF THE SAINTS

The Book of Revelation continues in a rather amazing way:

> When he broke the fifth seal, I saw underneath the altar the souls of all the people who had been killed on account of the Word of God, for witnessing to it. They shouted in a loud voice, "Holy, true Master, how much longer will you wait before you pass sentence and take vengeance for our death on the inhabitants of the earth?" Each of them was given a white robe, and they were told to be patient a little longer, until the roll was completed of their fellow-servants and brothers who were still to be killed as they had been. (6:9–11)

If we stop and think about this scripture, it is saying: "Wait a little longer, until the roll has been finished. The program hasn't been quite carried out yet, I have to kill a few more people."[11] What could this mean? Does it mean that God is subservient to a predetermined program? We find a similar passage in the apocryphal Jewish apocalypse usually called 4 Esra (but also called 2 Esdras). In the fourth chapter of that work, we are told that the "chambered" souls—souls of the dead waiting for their salvation—ask God: "How long are we to remain here?" They are getting impatient, just as the souls in Revelation are getting impatient. And the archangel's response is: "When the number of those like yourselves is completed; for [God] has weighed the age in the balance, and measured the times by measure, and numbered the times by number; and he will not move or arouse them until that measure is fulfilled" (New Revised Standard Version of the Apocrypha, 4:35–37). In other words, there is a pre-existing pattern in existence that God seems obliged to follow.

This corresponds to a remark of Jung in *Answer To Job*. He had been discussing Yahweh's considering the possibility of incarnating: yet "nothing can happen without a pre-existing pattern."[12] The comment reveals to what an extent Jung considers the archetypes—the ancient pre-existent patterns of the psyche—to be determinate. God himself can operate only through the patterns that are already laid down, an implication of our passage in Revelation: "You have to wait; the *pattern* requires that certain things be done first, that there be some more killings."

The question of vengeance comes up here: in the motive of revenge in the souls of those waiting under the divine altar and revenge even in the divine mind. It is something that Virgil brings up on the very first page of the *Aeneid:* "Can resentment so fierce dwell in heavenly breasts?"[13] There is, at any rate, no doubt that Yahweh is an "avenging" God. And I bring this up for reflection, because vengeance is so rampant in the psychology of the world today. Terrorist organizations of all kinds, and the cycles of revenge that go on and on, call out desperately for some psychological understanding of what is happening.[14] The issue is broached here in Revelation but is not without biblical antecedents. Let me demonstrate:

Deuteronomy 32:40–42:
Yes, I [Yahweh] raised my hand to heaven,
and I say, "As surely as I live for ever,
When I have whetted my flashing sword,
I shall enforce justice,
I shall return vengeance to my foes,
I shall take vengeance on my foes.
I shall make my arrows drunk with blood,
and my sword will feed on flesh:
the blood of the wounded
    and the prisoners,
the dishevelled heads of the enemy!"

Jeremiah 46.10:
For this is the Day of Lord
    Yahweh Sabaoth,
a day of vengeance
    when he takes revenge on his foes:
the sword will devour until gorged,
until drunk with their blood,
for Lord Yahweh Sabaoth
    is holding a sacrificial feast
in the land of the north,
    on the River Euphrates.

Nahum 1:2–6:
Yahweh is a jealous
   and vengeful God,
Yahweh takes vengeance,
   he is rich in wrath;
Yahweh takes vengeance on his foes,
he stores up fury for his enemies.
Yahweh is slow to anger
   but great in power,
Yahweh never lets evil
   go unpunished.
In storm and whirlwind
   he takes his way,
the clouds are the dust
   stirred by his feet.

The mountains tremble before him,
the hills reel;
the earth collapses before him,
the world and all who live in it.
His fury—who can withstand it?
Who can endure his burning wrath?
His anger pours out like fire
and the rocks break apart before him.

As I suggested at the beginning of this study, we can see from these Old Testament references that the Book of Revelation is largely Jewish with just a superficial Christian overlay. The vengeful deity is a far cry from the accepted doctrine of Christ and the Gospels. Indeed, as Jung explains in *Answer to Job,* the first Advent of Christ was meant to transform Yahweh; but the second Advent—with which the Book of Revelation is concerned—clearly brings back the untransformed God-image.

Here is what Jung says on this issue. He is writing about the sixth seal which we have yet to consider:

The sixth seal brings a cosmic catastrophe, and everything hides from the "wrath of the Lamb," "for the great day of his wrath is come." We no longer recognize the meek Lamb who lets himself be led unresistingly to the slaughter; there is only the aggressive and irascible ram whose rage can at last be vented. In all this I see less a metaphysical mystery than the outburst of long pent-up negative feelings such as can frequently be observed in people who strive for perfection.[15]

Here, Jung is explaining the imagery as having something to do with the personal psychology of John. But then he expands upon the notion:

> Let us be psychologically correct, however: it is not the conscious mind of John that thinks up these fantasies, they come to him in a violent "revelation." They fall upon him involuntarily with an unexpected vehemence . . . . I have seen many compensating dreams of believing Christians who deceived themselves about their real psychic constitution and imagined that they were in a different condition from what they were in reality. But I have seen nothing that even remotely resembles the brutal impact with which the opposites collide in John's visions . . . .
>
> The purpose of the apocalyptic visions is not to tell John, as an ordinary human being, how much shadow he hides beneath his luminous nature, but to open the seer's eye to the immensity of God, for he who loves God will know God. We can say that just because John loved God and did his best to love his fellows also, this "gnosis," this knowledge of God, struck him. Like Job . . . .[16]

The point is that conscious Christianity constructs a layer—I want to say a "veneer" so as to address the dubious aspects of it—over the individual psyche wherein the primordial Yahwistic libido has undergone a certain amount of transformation through education, experience, and the application of certain symbolic images consciously applied. However, break that veneer, scratch below it: and the primordial psyche is just as described in the passages we have read. Vengeance is a very prominent dynamism in the operation of the unconscious deriving from the *untransformed* Self. It is a grave problem for humanity, not to be glossed over by ineffectual preaching on Christian humility. Rather, as Jung states: "One does not become enlightened by imagining figures of light, but by making the darkness conscious."[17] That is what has the transformative effect. The darkness does not vanish but is mediated by a consciousness that knows its true nature.

Let me remind the reader that these texts from the Hebrew Bible and the New Testament give us a view of the facts of the objective psyche. They are not metaphysical facts, but psychic facts. And it does no good to fuss about whether they should or should not be a certain way—that is the way they are. Everyone who goes within deeply enough will discover these same facts, because they are a part of the collective psyche. We are all grounded in that same foundation.

STARS FALLING FROM HEAVEN

Although I cannot go into every aspect of symbolism in the Book of Revelation, I wish to call particular attention to the imagery of "stars falling from heaven" when the sixth seal is broken:

> In my vision, when he broke the sixth seal, there was a violent earthquake and the sun went as black as coarse sackcloth; the moon turned red as blood all over, and the stars of the sky fell onto the earth like figs dropping from a fig tree when a high wind shakes it; the sky disappeared like a scroll rolling up and all the mountains and islands were shaken from their places. Then all the kings of the earth, the governors and the commanders, the rich people and the men of influence, the whole population, slaves and citizens, hid in caverns and among the rocks of the mountains. They said to the mountains and the rocks, "Fall on us and hide us away from the One who sits on the throne and from the retribution of the Lamb. For the Great Day of his retribution has come, and who can face it?" (6:12–17) (See figure 4.3.)

"Stars falling from heaven" is an image of the "upper" or spiritual aspect of the collective unconscious erupting into consciousness. The "stars" would signify archetypal entities that fall down to "earth"; in other words, they fall into the ego. Thus, we have here an invasion of consciousness by the collective unconscious—which, as we have seen, is one of the features of the coming of the Self.

FIGURE 4.3

Albrecht Dürer. *The Opening of the Fifth and Sixth Seals, the Distribution of White Garments among the Martyrs, and the Fall of Stars.* ca.1498, Woodcut.

In *The Creation of Consciousness,* I have recorded a very impressive dream in this regard which we will take up below in greater detail; but at the beginning of it, the dreamer is standing on the Palisades, on the opposite side of the Hudson river from New York City, watching as Manhattan is invaded by giant aliens from outer space: and "fireballs were in the sky, heading for the earth."[18] That is a variation of the theme of stars falling from heaven. And I record another relevant dream in *Anatomy of the Psyche* in which a woman describes a piece of the moon falling down to earth into her apartment.[19] These are examples of how this basic image can express itself in the process of an analysis. But the image is also very common in the phenomenology of psychosis—when the collective unconscious bursts wide open and inundates the ego with transpersonal images that the ego cannot handle.

As our study proceeds, we will see that this invasion by the unconscious happens from two directions simultaneously: an invasion from "above" but also an invasion from "below." Both sets of images are directly applicable to what occurs psychologically when the unconscious starts to open up.

MARKED ON THE FOREHEAD

Now, let us consider at greater length the image of being "marked." It comes up in Revelation, chapter 7:

> Next I saw four angels, standing at the four corners of the earth, holding back the four winds of the world to keep them from blowing over the land or the sea or any tree. Then I saw another angel rising where the sun rises, carrying the seal of the living God; he called in a powerful voice to the four angels whose duty was to devastate land and sea. "Wait before you do any damage on land or at sea or to the trees, until we have put the seal on the foreheads of the servants of our God." And I heard how many had been sealed: a hundred and forty-four thousand, out of all the tribes of Israel. (7:1–4) (See figure 4.4; compare figure 6.3.)

The scripture explains that the number "a hundred and forty-four thousand" was reached by marking twelve thousand from each of

FIGURE 4.4

Sealing of the Saints. Wittenberg, 1522. Woodcut.

the twelve tribes of Israel—an allusion to the archetype of "Twelve."
Here is a close parallel from Ezekiel as the divine vengeance is
about to attack Jerusalem:

> Immediately six men advanced from the upper north gate, each hold-
> ing a deadly weapon. Among them was a man dressed in linen, with a

scribe's ink horn in his belt. They came in and halted in front of the bronze altar. The glory of the God of Israel rose from above the winged creature where it had been, towards the threshold of the Temple. He called to the man dressed in linen with a scribe's ink horn in his belt and Yahweh said to him, "Go all through the city, all through Jerusalem, and mark a cross on the foreheads of all who grieve and lament over all the loathsome practices in it." I heard him say to the others, "Follow him through the city and strike. Not one glance of pity; show no mercy; old men, young men, girls, children, women, kill and exterminate them all. But do not touch anyone with a cross on his forehead. (9:2–6)

This is the same idea of marking or sealing for the purpose of protection from divine vengeance. I should mention, however, that the translation of Hebrew *taw* as "cross" in this portion of Ezekiel is not followed universally; the New Revised Standard Version, for example, translates simply, "put a mark on the foreheads." It may be that the Roman Catholic background of the New Jerusalem Bible Version has influenced a translation with a Christian allusion. There is, however, some possibility that the early script for *taw* was cruciform.

The commentator for the Anchor Bible, J.M. Ford, makes an interesting speculation concerning the nature of this particular mark:

> It might be possible to connect the *taw* of salvation or preservation with the judicial proceedings involving the *Urim* and the *Thummin*, the objects, probably sacred lots, by which the priests gave an oracular decision in the name of Yahweh. These were set into the breastplate of the high priest (Exodus 39:8–21) but originally were small stones in the same size or shape but with different marks on them, such as *aleph* and *taw*, respectively the first and last letters of the Hebrew alphabet. In judicial proceedings the decision *aleph* would mean guilty ('*rr*, "to curse") and *taw* innocent (*tmm*, "to be blameless"). If the author of *Revelation* is influenced by this knowledge, the mark for the beast worshipers would be *aleph*.[20]

This "mark of the beast" appears later in our text; but here, we are concerned with its positive opposite, a "mark of salvation." If Ford's

comment holds, a developmental standard is implied by these
different marks associated with different letters. Symbolically, if
one has progressed all the way through the "psychological alphabet"—from beginning to the end—then one is marked out as
special.

The mark that Cain received when he went out into the world
amplifies this image of being sealed in a more ambiguous, mysterious way. He had killed his brother Abel and for his punishment was
banished from the land; but Cain remonstrated with Yahweh, "Why,
whoever comes across me will kill me!" And God replied:

> "Very well, then, . . . whoever kills Cain will suffer a sevenfold
> vengeance." So Yahweh put a mark on Cain so that no one coming
> across him would kill him. (Genesis 4:14–15)

Here, again, is the motif of "seven-fold." As well, the "mark" on Cain
is protective as in our Revelation scripture: Yet it is divine protection
for a murderer! I merely want to indicate how profoundly ambiguous these images are if one digs into them deeply enough. They
have dimensions of meaning that open up ambiguities not easily
resolved.

Another aspect of the positive seal is that it separates the "hundred and forty-four thousand" from the great multitude described
in the following verses ("a huge number, impossible for anyone to
count") who are still good enough to wear white robes and stand
before the throne of the Lord. This distinction can be understood
as the separation between the elect and the laity. All religious traditions distinguish between what is esoteric knowledge and what is
exoteric knowledge for those with different levels of development.
And so, again, a developmental scheme is implied.

The image of being "marked" comes up in dreams; and it is
almost always quite significant. I usually see it as an indication of
vocation, of being called for the individuation process. And one
may conclude that not very many people are called: out of an innumerable mass of human beings, only "a hundred and forty-four
thousand."

ROBES WASHED IN THE LAMB'S BLOOD

Our next item is the striking image of "robes being washed white in the blood of the Lamb." It appears in Revelation 7:13–15:

> One of the elders then spoke and asked me, "Who are these people, dressed in white robes, and where have they come from?" I answered him, "You can tell me, sir." Then he said, "These are the people who have been through the great trial; they have washed their robes white again in the blood of the Lamb. That is why they are standing in front of God's throne and serving him day and night in his sanctuary . . . ."

First of all, this is baptism imagery: after a baptism in Early Christianity, the neophyte was dressed in a white robe. So this scripture pertains to the symbolism of *solutio*—of alchemical "dissolution"—but of a peculiar and complex sort. For this is a baptism, not in water, but in blood. I have written an entire chapter on the symbolism of the "Blood of Christ" which can be found in *Ego and Archetype*.[21] And among the significant biblical references cited there is Genesis 49:10–11:

> The sceptre shall not pass from Judah,
> nor the ruler's staff from between his feet,
> until tribute be brought him
> and the peoples render him obedience.
> He tethers his donkey to the vine,
> to its stock the foal of his she-donkey.
> He washes his clothes in wine,
> his robes in the blood of the grape.

This is generally agreed to refer to the coming of the Messiah. And while it does not refer directly to "blood," "wine" as the "blood of the grape" is symbolically very close. Another relevant Messianic text appears in Isaiah 63:1–6:

> Who is this coming from Edom,
> from Bozrah in crimson garments,

so magnificently dressed,
marching so full of strength? . . .
—Why are your garments red,
your clothes like someone
treading the wine press?
—I have trodden the wine press alone;
of my people, not one was with me.
So I trod them down in my anger,
I trampled on them in my wrath.
Their blood squirted over my garments
and all my clothes are stained.
For I have decided on a day of vengeance,
a year of retribution has come.
I looked: there was no one to help me;
I was appalled but could find no supporter!
Then my own arm came to my rescue
and my own fury supported me.
I crushed the peoples in my anger,
I shattered them in my fury
and sent their blood streaming
to the ground.

Here, the scripture tells us of the coming Messiah's vengeance. According to these texts (which are the only ones that really use the imagery as we find it in the Book of Revelation), "washing one's robe in the blood of the Lamb" would mean to join in the slaughter of one's enemies. That is not the surface meaning: namely, that those "people who have been through the great trial" are the Christian martyrs victimized and bloodied by someone else's vengeance. The associated textual connections, however, suggest as a latent meaning precisely the opposite. This is another example of the ambiguity of imagery which comes to view when one looks beneath traditional expectations. Ford also considers it possible that those who have washed their robes in the blood of the Lamb are not just martyrs but have now "entered into battle alongside him as the warrior."[22]

There is, however, much we can learn from the usual interpretation of martyrdom. According to that understanding, those who have "washed their robes white in the blood of the Lamb" have shared in the sacrificial death of Christ by enduring a martyr's death for his name: thereby experiencing a baptism with the blood generated by the archetypal drama their martyrdom lived out. From a personal standpoint, a martyr's robe is washed in his or her own blood. But scripture states that these robes are washed in the "blood of the Lamb" or the "blood of Christ"—which means that the baptism or *solutio* taking place is an archetypal drama: the "blood" derives from the archetype of the Self. This, I believe, is the basic idea behind the image; because the martyrs did live out the fate of a timeless archetype. And it seems to be the idea behind Pascal's remark that "Jesus will be in agony even to the end of the world," an agony reliving itself all the time.[23]

The same motif can be found in the Gnostic doctrine of *Jesus patibilis* (Latin for "suffering Jesus"), one who is continually undergoing his sacrificial death in all of nature. He hangs on every tree, is served up in every dish, comes to life and dies daily—as the religious drama lives itself out everywhere, always. Psychologically speaking, that is a fairly accurate picture of the facts. I think this imagery refers to the fact that suffering—when experienced consciously as part of the archetypal drama of transformation—is redemptive. It is a participation in the Self-sacrifice of the God-image whereby the latter is transformed by virtue of the conscious participation of an ego that knows what is going on.[24]

Suffering itself has no value at all psychologically unless it is accompanied by the level of consciousness to which I refer. It may have some other value—political value, for example—but there is no redemptive psychological value without a consciousness of the archetypal context of the suffering. This is, of course, not an original thought but straight Jungian doctrine derived from Jung's *Answer to Job*.

5 Revelation: Chapters 8, 9, 10

THE INCENSE ALTAR

Chapter 8 of the Book of Revelation begins as follows:

> Next I saw seven trumpets being given to the seven angels who stand in the presence of God. Another angel, who had a golden censer, came and stood at the altar. A large quantity of incense was given to him to offer with the prayers of all the saints on the golden altar that stood in front of the throne; and so from the angel's hand the smoke of the incense went up in the presence of God and with it the prayers of the saints. (8:2–4)

We are confronted here with the significance of incense and the censer which dispenses it. The censer is that circular vessel on the end of a chain which the priest moves about to perfume the proceedings. As I mentioned above, the earthly tabernacle and its furnishings are a duplicate of what already exists in heaven—an arrangement for which a sketch is here provided (see figure 5.1). The square room (which is actually a cube) is the "Holy of Holies," containing the ark of the covenant with the mercy seat on its top, itself flanked by two huge cherubim. On the other side of the door or curtain—in what is still a "Holy Place" or sanctuary—is the lampstand, the table of consecrated "showbread," and an altar of incense. The brass basin or "sea," of which we have spoken, and the altar of burnt animal sacrifice are just outside these precincts. But the altar of incense, let us note, is within the nave of the Holy Place.

FIGURE 5.1

TABERNACLE

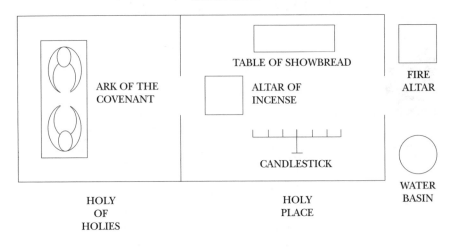

We find in Exodus quite explicit directions for its construction:

> "You will make an altar on which to burn incense; you will make it of
> acacia wood, one cubit long, and one cubit wide—it must be square—
> and two cubits high; its horns must be of a piece with it. You will over-
> lay its top, its sides all round and its horns with pure gold and make a
> gold moulding to go all round. . . . On it Aaron will burn fragrant
> incense each morning [it has been burning all night] . . . incense per-
> petually before Yahweh for all your generations to come." (30:1–8)

Further on in this chapter, the Lord tells Moses:

> Take sweet spices: storax, onycha, galbanum, sweet spices and pure
> frankincense in equal parts, and compound an incense, such a blend
> as the perfumer might make . . . . You will grind some of this up very
> fine and put it in front of the Testimony in the Tent of Meeting, where
> I shall meet you. You will regard it as especially holy. You may not make
> any incense of similar composition for your own use. You will regard it
> as holy, reserved for Yahweh. Anyone who makes up the same thing to
> be used as perfume will be outlawed from his people." (30:34–37)

In Leviticus, we learn how dangerous this incense altar and its censer can be. There had been a rebellion of two hundred and fifty priests against the authority of Moses; and so Moses proposed a religious test. They were to bring their censers to the tabernacle where Yahweh's "presence" resided: God would decide if he found their censing acceptable. And when they agreed to the test, fire shot out of the presence of Yahweh, destroying every last one of them in the midst of their censing. This event in the sacred history of the Israelites is referred to by the following scripture:

> Aaron's sons, Nadab and Abihu, each took his censer, put fire in it and incense on the fire, and presented unlawful fire before Yahweh, which was not in accordance with his orders. At this a flame leapt out from Yahweh's presence and swallowed them up, and they perished before Yahweh. Moses then said to Aaron, "That is what Yahweh meant when he said:
>
> > In those who are close to me
> > I show my holiness,
> > and before all the people I show my glory."
>
> Aaron remained silent. (10:1–3)

The reason why I am paying so much attention to this symbolism is that here we have the crucial psychological issue of transpersonal libido held in the hands of the ego. I assure the reader that this is not an antiquarian interest on my part. J.M. Ford also attends to this symbolism at some length. After referring to the "angel, who had a golden censer" (whom we have already seen), she quotes Revelation 8:5:

> Then the angel took the censer and filled it from the fire of the altar, which he then hurled down onto the earth; immediately there came peals of thunder and flashes of lightning, and the earth shook.

Ford comments about this verse:

> Four astonishing reversals occur. 1) From the throne and altar, whence one might expect mercy and atonement, comes wrath. 2) Incense,

which originally meant "fragrant smoke" . . . and was used with burnt offerings to be "a sweet savor to the Lord," a phrase repeated often in Leviticus, e.g., 1:13, 17, becomes an instrument of punishment. . . . The hurling of the coals is in rude opposition to the gentle rise of the cloud of incense, symbolizing prayer penetrating heaven and calling down God's mercy. 3) The trumpets, in association with the altar and throne, should suggest the instrument which was played during the pauses in the psalms . . . . Now the same instrument calls "Woe" and disaster. . . . Liturgy, conducted from heaven, brings destruction, not life.

Painting a picture of the earthly liturgy, this scholar continues:

One can recapture the scene of the daily sacrifice of incense offered in the temple . . . [which] took place in the morning after the lamb had been immolated but before it was placed on the altar of holocausts. The incense offering was repeated in the evening after the lamb was placed on the altar but before the libation. Accompanied by two other priests, the sacrificing priest, chosen by lot, entered the holy place. One of the assisting priests carried in a brazier burning coals which he had taken from the altar of holocausts with silver pincers. He placed the coals on the altar of incense, prostrated himself in adoration, and then retired. The celebrant took the incense from its container, which he handed to the second assisting priest, and poured the incense upon the coals. Then having inclined profoundly toward the holy of holies, he departed slowly, walking backwards in order to avoid turning his back on the altar. Finally, while the incense was burning, the priests prayed, and the sound of trumpets, interrupting the chanting of Psalm 150 by the Levites, announced to the people that they should join in adoration with the sacred ministers.[1]

All of this means that the burning coal in the censer of the priest who is offering incense to Yahweh is the earthly version of the "heavenly fire" described in the Book of Revelation. And it is heavenly fire granted by Yahweh under the very rigid prescription as to how it may be used. In Christian ecclesiastical terms, one could say that the operation of censing symbolizes the fact that the Church has at its disposal a certain amount of the sacred, divine fire granting it transpersonal authority: power over the flock of believers, and the authority to interpret the nature of God and how he should be worshipped. This corresponds to the idea that the Church has sole access to the Holy Spirit.

Psychologically, of course, we understand this symbolism as having to do with the individual's ego relationship to transpersonal libido. All of the scriptural injunctions surrounding it symbolize how carefully this libido must be handled. It is a very complex subject, because transpersonal libido does not come into one's life with a label around its neck, identifying itself as "transpersonal." It comes instead in those—often dangerously unrecognized—surges of special facility, creative inspiration, or special gifts and capacities.

Our passage in Revelation brings up the additional question: What is a censer doing in heaven? On earth, it is a form of subtle sacrifice in which incense is placed on a fire; and a fragrant smoke ascends to the nostrils of God in heaven. But what, then, is an incense altar doing above? It seems that the heavenly incense altar works in the reverse direction: instead of distributing the effects of the earthly fire upward, it moves downward, distributing divine fire onto the earth.

Fire Thrown to Earth

This, then, leads to the meaning in Revelation of "hurling fire down onto the earth." Let us note, first of all, that something similar happens in the Book of Ezekiel where Yahweh was making plans to punish Jerusalem by having her conquered by Babylonia. Sitting on his divine throne-chariot, he said to a "man dressed in linen": "Go in between the wheels below the winged creatures; take a handful of burning coal from between the winged creatures and scatter it over the city" (10:2). We find this same image of "fire falling from heaven" repeated elsewhere. Elijah overcame the false prophets of Baal by calling down divine fire to consume his sacrifice in a ritual competition; and, in that case, the divine energy was at the disposal of the prophet. Yahweh, of course, manifested himself to Moses in the fire of the burning bush. And even Christ announces in the Gospel of Luke, "I have come to bring fire to the earth" (12:49).

Furthermore, the imagery associated with transpersonal fire has a double aspect. As we shall see shortly, not only does fire fall from heaven, but smoke and fire rise up from the abyss when it opens up: heavenly fire and infernal fire, fire from two directions, and both of a transpersonal nature.

We frequently encounter this important image in dreams. "Fire" means affect. To the extent that it is transpersonal affect, it is undifferentiated transpersonal libido having its origin either in "heaven" or in "hell"—two realms in the psyche that are really not so far apart. They are two manifestations of the same psychic reality capable of shifting easily from one to the other. Now, in dreams, the outstanding example of transpersonal fire of mammoth proportions is a "nuclear explosion;" its magnitude links it to the apocalyptic imagery we are exploring. Smaller versions of this fire are found in the imagery of "lightning." We have an excellent example of that in Picture 2 of the mandala series Jung published in his essay, "A Study in the Process of Individuation" (see figure 5.2).[2] It depicts lightning coming down on a rocky landscape, blasting out a sphere from the surrounding hillside. And, as Jung explains, this is an image of blasting an individual psyche out of containment or identification with its containing matrix. It is the dramatic beginning of an individuation process—initiated by "divine fire." This is directly relevant to the imagery of fire coming down from heaven in the Book of Revelation.

SYMBOLISM OF ONE-THIRD

The text insists that we return now to number symbolism which appears with the sound of four battle trumpets (Rev. 8:6–12). With the blowing of the first: "a third of the earth was burnt up, and a third of all trees, and every blade of grass was burnt." With the blowing of the second: "a third of the sea turned into blood, a third of all the living things in the sea were killed, and a third of all ships were destroyed." When an angel blew the third trumpet: "a huge star fell from the sky, burning like a ball of fire, and it fell on a third of all rivers and on the springs of water . . . and a third of all water

FIGURE 5.2

Painting by an American woman patient, fifty-five years old, shown to C.G. Jung on the second day of her analysis. 1928. Watercolor.

turned to wormwood, so that many people died." And with the blowing of the fourth trumpet of war: "a third of the sun and a third of the moon and a third of the stars were blasted, so that the light went out of a third of them and the day lost a third of its illumination and likewise the night." Earlier in Revelation, we found ourselves assaulted by the archetype of "Seven" in many ways, then by the archetype of "Four" in the form of the four horsemen of the Apocalypse. Now, we have an assault by a weapon that divides things into "Three"—like a cookie cutter, stamping itself down on the earth in a variety of aspects to divide all things into thirds. It then eliminates one third of them.

As I have already suggested, "three" is the symbolic number of egohood, certainly if compared with the number "four." A three-fold process can be seen as a differentiating process in which the opposites manifest and then resolve themselves: number one is the original state; number two is the state of doubleness in conflict or opposition; and number three is the reconciliation of that conflict by a third position. Thus, the dynamic of thesis, antithesis, and synthesis is inherent in the imagery of the number three; so is the notion of right, left, and middle. In these expressions, we have the very principle of conscious experience: the way that ego consciousness organizes and understands its experience and its behavior. It follows that the assault of "three" in the imagery of Revelation means that the "earth" (each ego) is being forced into the full experience and living out of what it means to be conscious. Each individual is being asked to go through the process that separates the opposites, asked to endure the conflict that *separatio* brings, and then each is required to seek the resolution of separated opposites in the number "three."

I have a personal reason for trying to understand this. Many years ago, during a period of sizable psychic transition, I had a dream in a series I was to recognize in retrospect contained apocalypse imagery. My dream expressed the motif of the "destruction of one third":

A special ritual must be performed in order to allow the consecrated host of the communion meal to touch the ground. This is necessary because in the midst of the communion ceremony, a group of terrorists is going to burst in to the church and massacre one-third of the congregation. And when this happens, at this point, the officiating priest must drop the host to the ground and drop to the ground himself and protect the host with his body—the way a football player protects a fumbled football. And this must be done to protect the host from the possibility of blood's falling on it during the massacre.

It did not come to me right away, but eventually the massacre of "one third" of the congregation by terrorists associated in my mind to the imagery of the Apocalypse in the Book of Revelation. That clicked; that connection gave me my bearings to understand the dream. Here, then, is an example of how biblical imagery can be applied to a dream image: I believe the dream indicates that the sacred food of the Self—the "host"—which nourishes the ego during a moment of crisis must be grounded. Ordinarily, it would be a disaster for the host to be dropped during the communion ceremony.

And I think it is significant that about the time of my dream, Leonard Bernstein was producing his *Mass* in which the officiating priest has an accident and drops the elements. This work, which Bernstein calls a "Theatre Piece," has yet to receive the consideration it deserves; for it is very interesting on all levels, artistically and symbolically.[3] The point is that sacred entities must be grounded if they are to survive the apocalyptic encounter. They must be in touch with concrete, earthy, ambiguous reality—of the same nature, my dream suggests, as an ordinary football game.

In fact, during this period of my life, I found myself watching quite a bit of football on television. I wondered: "Why am I doing this? I'm really behaving like a mass man here." As I reflected, it dawned on me more and more to what extent *coniunctio* symbolism was playing itself out in these sporting contests and that what I was watching was really a degraded sacred ritual. Originally games were sacred rituals of the union of opposites; and the reader can find a short discussion of the psychology of sports in my work, *The Mystery of the Coniunctio*.[4] This, then, was one of my associations to the football imagery in my dream and one that brings a level of earthy reality to the experience of the sacred that it does not have in its elevated, remote position within the Mass itself.

It is also true that in the twenty-five years since I dreamed this symbolism, it has lived itself out in external reality. At the time, there had been no terrorists breaking into religious congregations in the midst of worship: But there have been since! And so I think that dream has a collective significance as well as a personal one, which is why I have referred to it. The danger, as the dream saw it, was that "blood" from the massacre would fall on the host. There is no explicit statement why that would be dangerous, but the implication is that the sacred entity would dissolve in a *solutio* of violence—that there would be some kind of catastrophic dissolution of the psychic core. I see this as imagery of how we should behave in these apocalyptic times: In the same way a football player protects a fumbled football, cover your precious, sacred value with everything you've got.

The Abyss Unlocked

We must now explore the "Abyss." It appears in the ninth chapter of the Book of Revelation:

> Then the fifth angel blew his trumpet, and I saw a star that had fallen from heaven onto the earth, and the angel was given the key to the shaft leading down to the Abyss. When he unlocked the shaft of the Abyss, smoke rose out of the Abyss like the smoke from a huge furnace so that the sun and the sky were darkened by the smoke from the Abyss, and out of the smoke dropped locusts onto the earth: they were given the powers that scorpions have on the earth . . . . (9:1–3) (See figure 5.3.)

Ford comments that in the Bible the English word "abyss" is used:

> to render the Hebrew word *tehom* about thirty times. *Tehom* has four meanings. It can signify the ocean which once spread over the earth but is not restricted to a subterranean abyss which is closed and sealed and accessible only through a shaft . . . . It can also mean the deep abode of Yahweh's enemy, the sea dragon . . . . A third meaning for *tehom* is earth, a pit which is a place of intermediate punishment . . . . Finally . . . *tehom* signified the temporary residence of fallen angels; it was a waterless, birdless, fiery place beyond the confines of earth and heaven, where the angels are in utter darkness and covered by rocks . . . .[5]

Biblically, there are overlapping terms here. The term "abyss"—translated literally as "the deep"—overlaps with the notion of "Hades," the land of the dead; and they both overlap associations with "Gehenna," which refers to a valley just south of Jerusalem where human sacrifices had once burned but where eventually the people just burned trash. Gehenna would stick in the mind as a "place of fiery punishment." Here, then, is another image that is

FIGURE 5.3

The Abyss is Opened and Locusts Emerge. Wittenberg, 1543. Woodcut.

immensely relevant to depth psychology; because it provides us with illustrations of how the psyche has described its own "depth." It is a description of the deep-seated unconscious, which has different aspects under different circumstances.

We are treated to yet another view of the Abyss by a Jewish legend of which I am quite fond; I referred to it in my chapter on King David in *The Bible and the Psyche.* And this version comes from Joseph Gaer's *The Lore of the Old Testament:*

> When King David's workmen began to build the House of God, they dug the drain for the altar very deep and inadvertently lifted the shard on the Mouth of the Abyss. Instantly, the Waters of the Deep began to rise to flood the earth. David knew that unless the Mouth of the Abyss were sealed again, the world would be destroyed. He also knew that only a stone with the Ineffable Name upon it could seal the Abyss

. . . . David lowered the stone with the Holy name on it sixteen thousand ells, and tightly sealed the Mouth of the Abyss. But it was soon discovered that the earth below had lost its moisture and even the rains were not enough to grow crops. King David then composed fifteen psalms, and as each psalm was completed, the Waters of the Deep rose one thousand ells. When the waters reached within a thousand ells of the surface of the earth, he offered thanks to God, Who keeps the ground always moist enough for crops, and does not allow the Abyss to sink one iota below, or rise one iota above, one thousand ells.[6]

The symbolism of being in danger of a flood from the Waters of the Deep—followed by the mistake of sealing the Abyss too far down so that the earth can no longer be moistened from below, while the rains from above are insufficient for life—is imagery worthy of a lengthy psychological discussion. I will leave it to the reader to reflect upon. Let it suffice for me to say that the "psalms" of David are so many occasions of active imagination; and they solve his problem.

In one of its several aspects, the Abyss is inhabited by fallen angels, demons, the transpersonal powers of darkness—by autonomous, unconscious complexes with archetypal cores. Indeed, autonomous, unconscious complexes that are rooted deeply are "demonic" entities; for they derive their energy from the untransformed primordial psyche. They are very real. Anyone who has undergone a significant personal analysis will have experienced at least minor "demonic possessions," a universal experience and one from which no one is immune. One's analysis can be superficial, of course. But should one require protection against demonic possession, only self-knowledge in depth provides it. When Jung was asked how he could live with the knowledge of the nature of God that he revealed to us in *Answer To Job,* he replied—as von Franz reports—"I live in my deepest hell and from there I can't fall any further."[7] This means that if one "lives" in that deepest hell the demonic complexes have undergone resolution: if the ego inhabits hell, it is no longer populated by unconscious demons; hell has been depopulated because penetrated by consciousness.

INVASION OF LOCUSTS

Our scripture tells us that when the shaft to the Abyss was unlocked, "smoke rose out of the Abyss like the smoke from a huge furnace." This is exactly the way that Yahweh manifested himself on Mount Sinai, and so the New Jerusalem Bible refers us in a footnote to Exodus 19:18 where we read:

> Mount Sinai was entirely wrapped in smoke, because Yahweh had descended on it in the form of fire. The smoke rose like smoke from a furnace and the whole mountain shook violently.

It is psychologically significant that the opening of the Abyss from "below" should be described as the theophany on Mount Sinai from "above" is described, because they are basically the same phenomenon viewed from different ego standpoints. At any rate, when the Abyss was opened, "out of the smoke dropped locusts onto the earth":

> These locusts looked like horses armoured for battle; they had what looked like gold crowns on their heads, and their faces looked human, and their hair was like women's hair, and teeth like lions' teeth. They had body-armour like iron breastplates, and the noise of their wings sounded like the racket of chariots with many horses charging. Their tails were like scorpions' tails, with stings, and with their tails they were able to torture people for five months. (Rev. 9:7–10)

Those are the "demonic powers." The imagery is not original but is borrowed from the Old Testament Book of Joel written in response to a "plague of locusts"—which the prophet interprets as an invading army on the great Day of Yahweh. Ford believes Joel is playing on words: the Hebrew word *hargol* for "locust" is close to the Arabic word *harjal* for "troops," a connection Near Eastern peoples would have picked up.[8] Here, then, is the relevant scripture:

> Listen to this, you elders;
> everybody in the country, attend!

Has anything like this ever happened in your day,
or in your ancestors' days?
Tell your children about it
and let your children tell their children,
and let their children the next generation!

What the nibbler has left, the grown locust has eaten,
what the grown locust has left, the hopper has eaten,
and what the hopper has left, the shearer has eaten. . . .

For a nation has invaded my country,
mighty and innumerable,
with teeth like a lion's teeth,
with the fangs of a lioness.
It has reduced my vines to a desolation
and my fig trees to splinters,
stripped them and broken them down,
leaving their branches white. . . .

The fields are ruined,
the land is in mourning,
for the grain has been ruined,
the new wine has failed,
of olive oil only a trickle. . . .

In their van a fire devours,
in their rear a flame consumes.
The country is like a garden of Eden ahead of them
and a desert waste behind them.
Nothing escapes them.
They look like horses,
like chargers they gallop on, . . .
Like fighting men they press forward,
like warriors they scale the walls,
each marching straight ahead,
not turning from his path; . . .
They hurl themselves at the city,

they leap onto the walls,
swarm up the houses,
getting in through the windows
like thieves. (Joel 1–2:9)

As a description of the Day of Yahweh, this is an invasion of the pent up demonic forces activated by the Apocalypse archetype; and, indeed, it is one of the ways that the collective unconscious can manifest itself.

Ford observes that the various plagues called down by the "trumpet blasts" have many parallels to the Old Testament plagues upon Egypt: one of them was thunder, hail, and fire which come with the first trumpet; another was that the Nile turned to blood, an aspect of the second trumpet; darkness over Egypt for three days corresponds to the fourth trumpet when one third of the light was lost; the plague of locusts was the eighth plague corresponding to the fifth trumpet we have just been examining; and a few other plagues have reversed parallels.[9] This indicates that the symbolism has come full circle, so to speak. It begins with Yahweh's imposition of plagues upon the Egyptians—the means by which the Israelites were freed from bondage and would eventually make their way to the promised land to found their nation. But, if we think of the Book of Revelation as essentially a Jewish apocalypse, the very same plagues that devastated Israel's enemy in the past are now applied to Israel herself.

I discuss the psychological meaning of each Egyptian plague in *The Bible and the Psyche*.[10] But, in general, we can understand them as responses from the unconscious against ego tyranny as represented by "Pharaoh." By ego tyranny, I mean the "God-almightiness" of an ego that perceives no ultimate inner, psychic agency other than itself. Something of a similar nature has called forth the same reaction in our apocalypse: in other words, the "Jews" have become "Egyptians."

Let me repeat, however, that this imagery of "invasion" really applies only to those individuals in whom there is a vast disparity between consciousness and the accumulated energies of the unconscious: a dissociated state which has built up such an intense polarization between these two psychic realms that this kind of imagery necessarily arises. And a civilization whose collective psyche has become thoroughly secularized—speaking psychologically, not religiously—that has lost all sense of connection to the transpersonal dimension of the psyche and of life is also fertile ground for the eruption of the same images. Since that is the state of our own civilization, it should not surprise us to hear the following modern dream:

> We're in a place like Central Park. The family's there, baby, too. The boy has taken on the features of a newborn chicken. No one seems to care though. Something else is going on. The ground's erupting, swelling with volcanic rumblings. There is a large, dark, bristling boil in the ground. Folks aren't overly concerned, however. It's a new volcano maybe, something for the six o'clock news. We gather what we have and move, but another similar eruption is occurring at the other end of the park. Confusion, fear, and wishes to remain stationary now grip the people. . . . other places in the world were now reporting eruptions, too. Eruptions here were growing louder—they were not from underground bombs but from the earth itself. Were they the result of "chance" or from something we had done in our relentless persecution of the earth's diversity? We ran for the car, drove homeward, but eruptions were becoming commonplace. Lights were fading; traffic jams occurred; the air was fouled with new debris and smoke; the drive became impossible; the baby cried. . . .[11]

Although this dream comes from Hill's collection of apocalyptic dreams, we might ask: What would an analyst do with such a dream if it were brought into a session? First of all, the analyst would investigate what was going on in the personal life of the dreamer; because dreams almost always have a personal level of reference, in addition to whatever other levels they may have. We cannot know what that personal material is in this case, but there clearly must be one. Yet it is also clear that this is more than a personal dream. Now, should someone ask me for exact criteria for determining when one is dealing with a collective dream, it is hard to be precise. But when I see the "shimmering" of an archetypal image shining through a dream—as in this case—then I know it is more than personal. And my knowledge and understanding of the collective Zeitgeist allows me to make a judgment as to whether or not the dream has some meaningful reference to contemporary collectivity. The collective component does not necessarily have a contemporary dimension to it, but in this case it most certainly does.

EATING OF THE SCROLL

In chapter 10 of Revelation, we encounter the strange image of "eating the small scroll":

> Then I heard the voice I had heard from heaven speaking to me again. "Go," it said, "and take that open scroll from the hand of the angel standing on sea and land." I went to the angel and asked him to give me the small scroll, and he said, "Take it and eat it; it will turn your stomach sour, but it will taste as sweet as honey." So I took it out of the angel's hand, and I ate it and it tasted sweet as honey in my mouth, but when I had eaten it my stomach turned sour. Then I was told, "You are to prophesy again, this time against many different nations and countries and languages and kings." (10:8–11) (See figure 5.4.)

This episode derives quite explicitly from a vision in Ezekiel:

> "But you, son of man, are to listen to what I say to you; do not be a rebel like that rebellious tribe. Open your mouth and eat what I am about to give you."
>
> When I looked, there was a hand stretching out to me, holding a scroll. He unrolled it in front of me; it was written on, front and back; on it was written, "Lamentations, dirges and cries of grief."
>
> He then, said, "Son of man, eat what you see; eat this scroll, then go and speak to the House of Israel." I opened my mouth; he gave me the scroll to eat and then said, "Son of man, feed on this scroll which I am giving you and eat your fill." So I ate it, and it tasted sweet as honey.
>
> He then said, "Son of man, go to the House of Israel and tell them what I have said." (2:8–3:4)

FIGURE 5.4

Albrecht Dürer. *St. John Devouring the Book.* 1497–1498. Woodcut.

Although this earlier text does not refer to a "sour taste," it is essentially the same image. The motif comes up commonly in dreams—not that one is asked to eat a book but that the dreamer is given something to eat. It means that some content is being offered by the unconscious to be "taken in" or assimilated by the ego.

The imagery is particularly striking because it also concerns the twofold symbolism of the "mouth."[12] On the one hand, the mouth is a receptive organ, taking in edible, nourishing material to assimilate it and turn it into one's own substance. On the other hand, the mouth is the expressive organ that emits the creative word. It is that twofold reference which gives us the symbolic linkage between "food" and "word," a connection that comes up repeatedly in the Bible where the Word of God is food. For example:

Deuteronomy, 8:3:
He humbled you, he made you feel hunger, he fed you with manna which neither you nor your ancestors had ever known, to make you understand that human beings live not on bread alone but on every word that comes from the mouth of Yahweh.

Proverbs, 9:5 where Wisdom says:
Come and eat my bread,
drink the wine which I have drawn!

Ecclesiasticus, 15:2–3 speaking of Wisdom:
She will come to meet him like a mother,
    and receive him like a virgin bride.
She will give him the bread of understanding to eat,
    and the water of wisdom to drink.

In these passages, the two aspects of mouth symbolism are combined: the word coming out of the mouth of Yahweh or Sophia is taken into the mouth of the recipient as food to be digested. The prophet, then, was evidently supposed to regurgitate that word and express it again from his mouth. For, in the passages from Revelation and Ezekiel, no sooner was the prophet instructed to eat the scroll than he was instructed to go out and preach what was in it. This leaves open the question whether or not what is being preached has been assimilated first of all by the preacher since some people behave the way that birds feed their young. It is a question to ask when confronted by apparent prophets claiming to give expression to transpersonal truths: Are they regurgitating what has been assimilated or merely mouthing what has scarcely been taken in?

6 Revelation: Chapters 11, 12, 13

MEASURING THE TEMPLE

Chapter 11 opens with a rather strange image. We read:

> Then I was given a long cane like a measuring rod, and I was told, "Get up and measure God's sanctuary, and the altar, and the people who worship there; but exclude the outer court and do not measure it, because it has been handed over to gentiles. . . ." (11:1–2)

Here we learn of the significance of "measuring" which deserves some attention. As with so much of the material in the Book of Revelation, this imagery has a prototype found in other visionary books and especially in the Book of Ezekiel. There, in chapter 40, Ezekiel describes another one of his visions while living in exile:

> the hand of Yahweh was on me. He carried me away: in divine visions, he carried me away to the land of Israel and put me down on a very high mountain, on the south of which there seemed to be built a city. He took me to it, and there I saw a man, whose appearance was like brass. He had a flax cord and a measuring rod in his hand and was standing in the gateway. The man said to me, "Son of man, look carefully, listen closely and pay attention to everything I show you, since you have been brought here only for me to show it to you. Tell the House of Israel everything that you see." (40:1–4)

What follows is a very lengthy description in which Ezekiel watches this man measure out a temple, with all the dimensions made clear.

In some Bibles (for instance, the NIV Study Bible), diagrams are provided of this visionary temple that has been described so precisely that it can be drawn—even though it never existed. Let us remind ourselves that at the time of Ezekiel's visions the temple at Jerusalem had already been destroyed in 586 B.C.E.; there was no temple there, and the elite of Jewish culture were living in captivity. Likewise, at the time of John's vision, the temple had been destroyed yet again by Titus in 70 C.E.; and it has never been rebuilt. So, we learn here that John is being told to measure, not an actual concrete temple, but a visionary one.

Now that is a strange sort of business: to apply the precise approach of quantitative measuring to visionary subject matter. And, as with all this material, the question arises: What does it mean? Measuring is a careful, rational, analytic procedure in preparation for some actual construction. Therefore, John (uncharacteristic of his usual role) has become at this moment an active participant in the divine drama; he is not just a passive recipient. True enough, the moment passes, but it appears here. I see it as evidence of the psychological fact that the ego must actively participate in understanding and completing the purposes of the unconscious, once the unconscious is activated. The ego must participate in the construction of the "temple" of the Self—it does not just happen miraculously while the ego passively looks on. In that regard, I remind the reader of the Max Zeller dream cited above in which various people are working on the construction of an extraordinary temple.[1]

The Sun-Moon Woman

The next vision is perhaps the most important in the whole Book of Revelation, considered psychologically. Beginning in chapter twelve, we read:

> Now a great sign appeared in heaven: a woman, robed with the sun, standing on the moon, and on her head a crown of twelve stars. She was pregnant, and in labour, crying aloud in the pangs of childbirth.

Then a second sign appeared in the sky: there was a huge red dragon with seven heads and ten horns, and each of the seven heads crowned with a coronet. Its tail swept a third of the stars from the sky and hurled them to the ground, and the dragon stopped in front of the woman as she was at the point of giving birth, so that it could eat the child as soon as it was born. The woman was delivered of a boy, the son who was to rule all the nations with an iron sceptre, and the child was taken straight up to God and to his throne, while the woman escaped into the desert, where God had prepared a place for her to be looked after for twelve hundred and sixty days. (12.1-6) (See figure 6.1.)

Although extraordinarily important, this passage is something of a foreign body in the text. With the exception of the one phrase—"the son who was to rule all the nations with an iron scepter"—there are no biblical references. In other words, the events described here take place outside the tapestry or the fabric of interconnected allusions that make up the rest of the book. The focus, of course, is upon a figure we might call the "Sun-Moon Woman"—the woman so intimately connected to these two celestial bodies that she is clothed in the sun while her feet rest upon the moon. Although the strain in conventional interpretations is evident, the most common view is that she represents the "community" of God's people. Thus, if one interprets her from the standpoint of Judaism, she is the community of Israel; if one's standpoint is Christianity, she represents the community of the Church. In either case, the child is commonly considered to be the Messiah even though—in the case of Christ—the Anointed One had already been born long before the time of this vision. Sometimes, commentators equate the "Sun-Moon Woman" with Mary, the mother of Jesus, so that the child's being caught up to heaven immediately after his birth can be taken somehow as the Ascension of Christ as a fully-grown man. All of this commentary exhibits a straining to make things fit. An interesting variation, however, appears in current Jehovah's Witnesses theology: namely, that the "Sun-Moon Woman" is Jehovah's symbolic wife—a somewhat surprising notion coming from a fundamentalist sect!

Jung attributes great significance to this imagery in the Book of Revelation, and he comments as follows:

FIGURE 6.1

The Woman of the Apocalypse, from *the Cloisters Apocalypse.* ca. 1310–1320.
Illumination. The Cloisters Collection, Metropolitan Museum of Art, New York.

This vision is altogether out of context. Whereas with the previous
visions one has the impression that they were afterwards revised,
rearranged, and embellished, one feels that this image is original and
not intended for any educational purpose. . . . for it is all part of the
heavenly *hieros gamos,* whose fruit is a divine man-child. He is threat-
ened with the fate of Apollo, the son of Leto, who was likewise pursued
by a dragon.[2]

Indeed, this imagery is a clear reference to the Greek myth of Leto who gave birth to Apollo and Artemis. Zeus had sexual relations with Leto who became pregnant with twins—arousing the jealousy of Hera who persecuted her rival. She directed the dangerous Python to follow Leto and denied permission, in effect, for any country to give her rest in order to give birth. No country would accept her. And so eventually Apollo and Artemis were born on the floating island of Delos, which did not quite "exist" since it was merely floating. Shortly after the birth (upon which event the island took root and became substantial), the young Apollo slew Python, his mother's enemy.

The parallel with our apocalypse is very close. Leto is intimately related to the sun and moon since she really gives birth to this celestial pair: the anthropomorphic pair "Apollo-Artemis" implied for the Greeks, at the cosmic level, "sun-moon." That means—shifting to alchemical terms—that the Sol-Luna *coniunctio* existed on an unconscious basis in the dark womb of Leto before the births; when her children were born, a *separatio* took place in the distinction of celestial bodies and in the distinction of deities. This process, therefore, was happening within the psyche of the Greeks at that stage of their development. Yet, look at what happens in Revelation: the Sun-Moon Woman is associated with the same heavenly bodies as already distinct separate entities, being clothed with the sun while standing upon the moon; and she gives birth not to twins but to a single child. There is, then, something of a reverse-parallel to the story of Leto whereby the child in Revelation represents a union of the opposites that had previously separated.

Jung himself alludes to this interpretation in *Answer to Job:*

> The son who is born of these heavenly nuptials is perforce a *complexio oppositorum,* a uniting symbol, a totality of life. John's unconscious, certainly not without reason, borrowed from Greek mythology in order to describe this strange eschatological experience, for it was not on any account to be confused with the birth of the Christ-child which had occurred long before under quite different circumstances.[3]

Since the child born in Revelation is "taken up" ("caught up" is the way most translations put it) to God and his throne, Jung felt moved to state:

> This would seem to indicate that the child-figure will remain latent for an indefinite time and that its activity is reserved for the future.[4]

I think we could say that this particular visionary episode embedded in the very middle of the Apocalypse of John is the living heart of the entire vision, understood psychologically. It is buried, as a relatively quiet little episode, in the midst of all the sound and fury of the apocalypse. This passage in chapter 12 is clearly an authentic spontaneous expression of *coniunctio* symbolism and even demonstrates its authenticity by the fact that it sits outside the elaborate fabric of textual parallels containing the rest of the text. And the very fact that this imagery derives from a pagan source further verifies its psychological authenticity. Jung says as much:

> The fact that John uses the myth of Leto and Apollo in describing the birth may be an indication that the vision, in contrast to the Christian tradition, is a product of the unconscious. But in the unconscious is everything that has been rejected by consciousness, and the more Christian one's consciousness is, the more heathenishly does the unconscious behave, if in the rejected heathenism there are values which are important for life—if, that is to say, the baby has been thrown out with the bath water, as so often happens.[5]

Indeed, the supreme value is to be found embedded in this Greek or so-called heathen imagery; because it is the symbol of wholeness. It is the image of totality, the *coniunctio:* That is the "baby."

WAR IN HEAVEN

We must now consider the theme of "war in heaven" and the subsequent casting of Satan out of his heavenly abode and down to earth. These events appear also in chapter 12 of Revelation:

> And now war broke out in heaven, when Michael with his angels attacked the dragon. The dragon fought back with his angels, but they

were defeated and driven out of heaven. The great dragon, the primeval serpent, known as the devil or Satan, who had led all the world astray, was hurled down to the earth and his angels were hurled down with him. Then I heard a voice shout from heaven, "Salvation and power and empire for ever have been won by our God, and all authority for his Christ, now that the accuser, who accused our brothers day and night before our God, has been brought down. . . . So let the heavens rejoice and all who live there; but for you, earth and sea, disaster is coming—because the devil has gone down to you in a rage, knowing that he has little time left." (12:7–12)

Psychologically, this is exceedingly interesting. For it is only now—at the moment John is witnessing his vision—that the decisive split occurs in the pleroma (which is to say, in the unconscious) between the two sides of the Godhead. Finally, the "persecutor" has been cast out of heaven down to earth; and there has occurred within the divine entity a split between good and evil. Or, to use Jung's terminology, Satan—the second son of Yahweh—has been born. Yet Christ, the first-born son of Yahweh, had already announced this event decades earlier in Luke, where he reports: "I watched Satan fall like lightning from heaven" (10:18). Either that was a premonitory vision or, on some level, the event had already taken place.

Milton's great poem, *Paradise Lost,* relies upon the Judeo-Christian legend that Satan had been cast out of heaven even earlier—namely, prior to the Fall of Adam and Eve—and that Satan had been living as a serpent in the Garden of Eden. The sixth chapter of Genesis alludes to the sinful union of the "sons of God" with mortal women on the earth in earliest times; while the Book of Enoch expands considerably on the theme that there were "fallen angels" in the days of Noah. The image, as we can see, is exceedingly fluid; it floats around in history and can come to rest here, there, and yonder. Let us read from Milton who has already spoken in his poem of Adam and Eve's Fall:

Who first seduc'd them to that foul revolt?
Th' infernal Serpent; hee it was, whose guile
Stirr'd up with Envy and Revenge, deceived
The Mother of Mankind; what time his Pride

Had cast him out from Heav'n, with all his Host
Of Rebel Angels, by whose aid aspiring
To set himself in Glory above his Peers,
He trusted to have equall'd the most High,
If he oppos'd; and with ambitious aim
Against the Throne and Monarchy of God
Rais'd impious War in Heav'n and Battle proud
With vain attempt. Him the Almighty Power
Hurl'd headlong flaming from th' Ethereal sky
With hideous ruin and combustion down
To bottomless perdition, there to dwell
In Adamantine Chains and penal Fire,
Who durst defy th' Omnipotent to Arms. (1:33–49)[6]

This is exactly the same image as in the Book of Revelation, yet set at the very beginning of human history by Milton who was following the ecclesiastics of his day. But this early placement does not fit the canonical scriptures in the least, as the Book of Job makes very clear and as Rivkah Kluger demonstrates in her book, *Satan in the Old Testament*.[7] Satan had access to heaven throughout the Old Testament period. He had not yet been cast out of heaven but could come and go.

It is, nevertheless, most interesting that Milton should write his classic account of this archetypal image at the particular time that he did. He wrote in the seventeenth century; and—as I understand it and Jung indicates in *Aion*—Satan did "fall out of heaven" empirically at the beginning of the sixteenth century with the visible advent of the Anti-Christ and, incidentally, with the emergence of the legend of Faust's encounter with Mephistopheles. Another way of putting it is that the God-image "fell" out of metaphysical projection about 1500 C.E. for the creative minority of Western humanity. And by lodging itself in the vicinity of the ego, the positive image of "Lucifer" (Latin for "light-bearing") reversed its polarity. This shift was due to the fact that whenever transpersonal energies touch the ego, they generate inflation: they become "Luciferian" in the negative sense.[8]

Let us listen again, this time from the Authorized or King James Version, how heaven reacts to the casting out of Satan:

> Therefore rejoice, ye heavens and ye that dwell in them. Woe to the inhabiters of the earth and of the sea! for the devil is come down unto you, having great wrath, because he knoweth that he hath but a short time. (KJV, 12:12)

This verse indicates that "heaven" (the collective unconscious) is cleansing itself of a troublesome character and fobbing it off on the "earth" (symbolic of the ego). And that, indeed, is what has happened in the last five hundred years of the Christian aeon. There has been a vast expansion of conscious human energies and initiatives in all areas of human enterprise. This has been accompanied by progressive ego inflation. It is a characteristic of our times that has reached such proportions that scarcely anyone can disregard it.

There is a striking association to all this in William Blake's *Illustrations of the Book of Job.* I have written a small book on that series of twenty-two engravings which pretty much follow the biblical account.[9] Engraving fifteen, for example, depicts Yahweh pointing out to Job the "Behemoth" that the Lord had created (Job 40:15); and we can interpret this monster as the "underside" of God (see figure 6.2). But engraving sixteen is another matter. It depicts Satan being thrown out of heaven, down into hell, even below the earth: and yet this event occurs nowhere in the Book of Job! So, the question is: What is that image doing in Blake's series? It is as though the unconscious of this artist—with uncanny perspicacity—slipped in this image precisely at that point because that is where Job discovered consciously the two sides of Yahweh's nature. At that moment of *discrimination,* Yahweh and Satan got "separated." I find this quite a remarkable example of how the authentic psyche can reveal itself to a creative artist when the artist is dealing with the kind of material that allows for revelation (see figure 6.3).

FIGURE 6.2

William Blake. *Behold now Behemoth which I made with thee,* from *Illustrations of the Book of Job.* Watercolor.

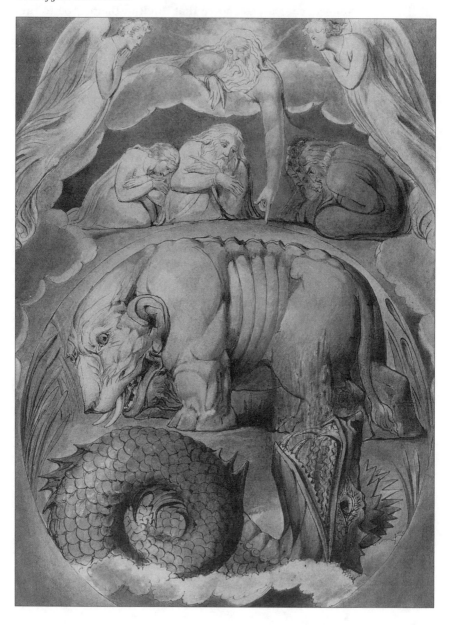

FIGURE 6.3

William Blake. *Thou hast fulfilled the Judgment of the Wicked,* from *Illustrations of the Book of Job.* Watercolor.

THE BEASTS

We read in chapter 13 of the Book of Revelation:

> Then I saw a beast emerge from the sea: it had seven heads and ten
> horns, with a coronet on each of its ten horns, and its heads were
> marked with blasphemous titles. I saw that the beast was like a leopard,
> with paws like a bear and a mouth like a lion; the dragon had handed
> over to it his own power and his throne and his immense authority. . .
> . Then I saw a second beast, emerging from the ground; it had two
> horns like a lamb, but made a noise like a dragon. This second beast
> exercised all the power of the first beast. . . . (13:1–2, 11–12) (See fig-
> ure 6.4.)

While there are important particulars worth examining here, I must
concentrate upon the overall meaning of the two "beasts" which
carry the major psychological content of this section. According to
many scholars, these two beasts are the biblical monsters Leviathan
and Behemoth. Leviathan is the sea monster ("from the sea"); and
Behemoth is the land monster ("from the ground"). It is, in fact,
true that when the Apocalypse archetype is activated and the unconscious opens up, the coming of the Self—with all its tumultuous
phenomena—brings with it not only "spiritual" but also "animal"
transpersonal energies. As a modern dreamer reports: "So much
heat had been generated deep down into the earth from the atomic
bomb explosions that earthquakes forced long dormant dinosaur
eggs to the surface, where they hatched."[10] That is a nearly precise
modern parallel to this motif of the apocalyptic appearance of
"monsters."

These two creatures, Leviathan and Behemoth, appear first
of all in the Book of Job. Yahweh is answering Job out of the whirlwind and says:

> Brace yourself like a fighter,
>   I am going to ask the questions and you are to inform me!
> Do you really want to reverse my judgment,
>   put me in the wrong and yourself in the right?

FIGURE 6.4

Albrecht Dürer. *The Sea Monster and the Beast.* ca. 1498. Woodcut.

Has your arm the strength of God's,
    can your voice thunder as loud?
Come on, display your majesty and grandeur,
    robe yourself in splendour and glory
Let the fury of your anger burst forth,
    humble the haughty at a glance!
At a glance, bring down all the proud,
    strike down the wicked where they stand.
Bury the lot of them in the ground,
    shut them, everyone, in the Dungeon.
And I shall be the first to pay you homage,
    since your own right hand is strong enough to save you.
But look at Behemoth, my creature, just as you are! . . .

Leviathan, too! Can you catch him with a fish-hook
or hold his tongue down with a rope? (40:7–14, 25)

As part of his overpowering manifestation, God brings out for Job to witness what Jung calls his "menagerie." These are images of the primordial psyche. They are the "underside" of Yahweh—or, as Jung puts it, the "abysmal world of shards." In the Apocalypse of John, they come into overt manifestation for all to see. Again and again, we are exposed to the event of transpersonal energies "invading" the ego: heavenly energies fall out of heaven; demonic spiritual energies rise up from their confinement in hell; and brute animal energies emerge from the sea and the earth into visibility.

The symbolic presence of Behemoth and Leviathan in Revelation establishes a connection with the Book of Job; and that helps us to understand better why Jung chose to discuss these texts together in his *Answer to Job*. The first half of that work is indeed about the Old Testament Book of Job; but the last portion is about the New Testament Book of Revelation. The symbolic continuity is clear: Job's individual ordeal was a kind of prelude to the collective ordeal pictured by the Apocalypse. And just as Jung's *Answer To Job* provides us with the meaningful understanding of Job's ordeal, it also helps us to understand the apocalyptic events pictured in the

Book of Revelation. Furthermore, just as Jung's work helps us to understand what is going on when one of us has an individual "Job" ordeal, it helps us to grasp the meaning of the apocalyptic events going on today in the collective psyche—events in which we find ourselves engaged, at the very least, as participant-observers.

Indeed, I think that the significance of Jung's brief work, *Answer to Job,* cannot be overestimated. No other source provides insight into the meaning of the Jewish Holocaust—as just one example of the Apocalypse that is now going on in the collective psyche. And it *is* going on. Once one gets some awareness of the relevant symbolism, then one is able to see it; there is no need for any great prophetic powers, because the events are already visible. All one has to do is look below the surface and see what is happening at the level of the collective psyche. Of course, it does require a little work to understand what Jung is talking about.

According to the apocryphal Syrian Apocalypse of Baruch, "Leviathan shall rise from the sea with the advent of the Messiah."[11] This same source states that Behemoth also shall be revealed and that both monsters shall become "food" for the survivors of the End. Jewish legend elaborated this theme quite beautifully. It is a theme I consider of sizable psychological importance, and I have already discussed it in *The Bible and the Psyche.*[12] According to legend, there will be a great Messianic Banquet at which the flesh of Behemoth and Leviathan will be eaten and the Garden of Eden will be restored. Raphael Patai quotes one legend in his *Messiah Texts* as follows:

> In that hour the Holy One, blessed be He, will set tables and slaughter Behemoth and Leviathan . . . and prepare a great banquet for the pious. And He will seat each one of them according to his honor . . . . And the Holy One, blessed be He, will bring them wine that was preserved in its grapes since the six days of creation. . . . And He fulfills the wishes of the pious, rises from the Throne of Glory, and sits with them . . . . And He brings all the fine things of the Garden of Eden. . . . .[13]

Farther on we learn:

> And the Holy One, blessed be He, will expound to them the meanings
> of a new Torah which He will give them through the Messiah. . . . In
> that hour the Holy One, blessed be He, takes the keys of Gehenna
> and, in front of all the pious, gives them to Michael and Gabriel, and
> says to them: "Go and open the gates of Gehenna, and bring them up
> from Gehenna. . . ." And Gabriel and Michael stand over them [the
> wicked] in that hour, and wash them, and anoint them with oil, and
> heal them of the wounds of Gehenna, and clothe them in beautiful
> and good garments, and take them by their hand, and bring them
> before the Holy One, blessed be He . . . .[14]

Is that not a refreshingly different version of what we have been
reading in our Christian apocalyptic text? In this Jewish legend, we
have an image of reconciliation, the emergence of authentic totality. Except for the mandala vision at the end of the Book of
Revelation, we have instead in the main body of the Christian material a whole series of very violent *separatio* images. That has to be
understood as a necessary psychological process required for the
stage of development of the collective psyche reflected in the text.
But the idea of a "Messianic banquet" suggests that the primordial
psyche *is* going to be assimilated.

THE NUMBER 666

Chapter 13 of Revelation goes on to speak of the requirement that
the "Beast" be worshipped in the Last Days; and there are clear references here to Late Roman Emperors who did claim personal
divinity. In addition, beast-worshippers were to be branded with the
name of the beast or with the number equivalent of its name (see
figure 6.5; compare figure 4.4).

Scripture states: "There is need for shrewdness here: anyone
clever may interpret the number of the beast: it is the number of a
human being, the number 666" (13:18). Now, some readers may
recall Jung's remark in *Mysterium Coniunctionis* that the alchemical
"Enigma of Bologna" acted like "flypaper for every conceivable projection that buzzed in the human mind"—attracting to it a great
many different interpretations throughout the centuries.[15] Well,

FIGURE 6.5

Marked by the Beast. Illumination. Bodleian Library, Oxford.

this image—the "number of the Beast, 666"—is also psychic flypaper, generating innumerable projections for centuries. Groups uniformly have projected their enemies onto the number 666; and they did that because in antiquity letters of the alphabet were equivalent to numbers (the first letter is number one, the second letter is number two, and so forth). One could also juggle around the name of a person—put it in Latin or Greek or Hebrew or in a combination of languages until the number came up "right." It was not too hard to do. But of the projections that have landed on this apocalyptic "fly-paper" over the centuries, none was more frequent than the name of the Roman Emperor Nero. The phrase "Nero Caesar" was considered to add up to "666"; but other persecuting Caesars were also brought into this symbolism. Certain Christian Fathers thought the number somehow referred specifically to the Gnostic Ogdoad ("eightfold"), because the Gnostics were their greatest enemy. When the Reformation arrived in sixteenth-century Europe, Protestants thought the number 666 referred to their nemesis, the Catholic Church; indeed, when they referred to the Church as "Italika Ekklesia," the infamous number would suspiciously emerge.[16] If Protestants called the Pope in Greek, "Papeiskos," the alphabet-number system would work out perfectly. Of course, the Catholic Church returned the favor and applied this system to their enemy Luther. All Christians applied the alphabet-number symbolism to Muḥammed—and in more recent times to Napoleon and, finally, to Hitler.[17]

I have nothing more to say about this number as a total but wish to reflect upon it as a triplicate of the number "six" which is clearly emphasized. Traditionally, the number six has been chiefly known as the "marriage" number. And the symbolic "reason" for that is—keeping in mind that symbolic reasons do not follow the same logical pathway as does rationality—that it is the product or "marriage" of the first two prime numbers, two and three. Another more cogent reason, I think, is that it represents the "union" of a pair of triads signified geometrically by two triangles. This imagery was used in alchemy: the upward-pointing triangle is the sign for "fire"; and the downward-pointing triangle is the sign for "water." When they are superimposed—"married"—then one gets the so-called Solomon's Seal, popularly referred to as the six-pointed Star of David (see figure 6.6).

There is nothing obviously negative about that symbolism surrounding the number "six" which would lend itself to the infernal character of "666." But, if we consider what is likely to happen when fire and water come together (when we focus upon the conflict that

FIGURE 6.6

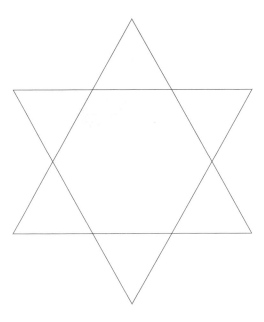

is likely to be generated) then this number can indeed turn negative. I also think of the number six as an image of the *coniunctio*
under the aegis of the number "three," which is the aegis of the
ego.[18] The ego as "light-bringer" associates, of course, to the ambiguity of "Lucifer." Yet another way of accounting for the negative
nuance can be found in traditional quaternity thinking. In the first
number series (1, 2, 3, 4), two is considered "demonic." That is due
to the fact that this number generates the notion of the "other,"
which has a sinister component. We can observe this otherwise
obscure symbolism in our words "duplicity," "double-cross," and
even "doubt"—all of which are cognate with a questionable
"twoness." And something similar can be said of the number six in
the second quaternity series (5, 6, 7, 8). It occupies the same relative position as does the number two and even alludes to the second
triangle in "conflict" with the first. These reflections may seem too
speculative to the reader—who is free to dismiss their symbolic
logic—yet this is the kind of thinking that the imagery induces

FIGURE 6.7

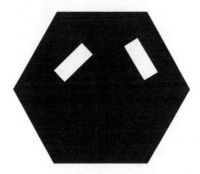

when one attempts to understand why the number six is so "diabolical" in the Book of Revelation.

Finally, I offer a personal experience. When I was working on my book, *Ego and Archetype,* I had on my desk the image of a hexagon that was part of a dream I was interpreting. And one day, when my eight-year-old daughter came by and saw it, she shuddered. The hexagon with two rectangles cut out of it like windows near the top looked something like a primitive mask: indeed, I suggest, a six-sided mask of the "dark deity." This is another allusion to the sinister aspect of the number six (see figure 6.7).[19]

7 Revelation: Chapters 14, 15, 16

FIRST FRUITS

At the very beginning of chapter fourteen, we read:

> Next in my vision I saw Mount Zion, and standing on it the Lamb who had with him a hundred and forty-four thousand people, all with his name and his Father's name written on their foreheads. I heard a sound coming out of heaven like the sound of the ocean or the roar of thunder; it was like the sound of harpists playing their harps. There before the throne they were singing a new hymn in the presence of the four living creatures and the elders, a hymn that could be learnt only by the hundred and forty-four thousand who had been redeemed ["purchased"] from the world. These are the sons who have kept their virginity and not been defiled with women; they follow the Lamb wherever he goes; they, out of all people, have been redeemed to be the first-fruits for God and for the Lamb. (14:1–4)

I wish to focus here upon the image of "first fruits" as it appears in association with "one hundred and forty-four thousand" people. This large number can be considered as the "apotheosis" of the number twelve: it is twelve squared times a thousand, so it is the number twelve raised to higher and higher levels and thus a number of "totality." According to scripture, this is the total of elect martyrs who have been sacrificed for following the Lamb, which itself has been sacrificed. But the issue has to do with "first fruits," a most interesting theme in the Old Testament. Yahweh states explicitly that the first fruits of all harvests (including the first fruit of the human womb) belong to him. They are to be sacrificed to God. Should one neglect that requirement—should one eat the first fruits or hold back a beloved first child rather than hand them over to Yahweh for his meal—then one is inviting disaster. And that is stated explicitly in the second chapter of Jeremiah: "Israel was sacred to Yahweh;/the first-fruits of his harvest;/all who ate this incurred guilt,/disaster befell them" (2:3). Symbolically, the idea is that the first fruits are God's food; and if he is not given his meal voluntarily, then he takes it by violence.

But in the early history of Israel, at the time of the Exodus, the Egyptians bore the brunt of this phenomenon. Their first-born were killed as "first fruits," says the Bible. Since they had not made a sacrifice voluntarily, what was required was taken involuntarily. The pattern even repeats itself on the divine level, because the "first fruit" of Yahweh is his "only-begotten" son Jesus Christ; and yet he is sacrificed to the Father. I cannot say exactly why this should be so, but the requirement cuts through many levels of the psyche. And it does seem to be true that in human experience, very commonly, the "first-born" in a family has a different psychology from that of later siblings as does an only child in relation to other children. There appears to be a different relationship to the transpersonal dimension of the unconscious, a relationship that is more problematic. Whatever the meaning or purpose, this pattern appears to be an archetypal fact.

The Eternal Gospel

Next we read in our Apocalypse:

> Then I saw another angel, flying high overhead, sent to announce the gospel of eternity to all who live on the earth, every nation, race, language and tribe. He was calling, "Fear God and glorify him, because the time has come for him to sit in judgement; worship the maker of heaven and earth and sea and the springs of water." (14:6–7)

Here, the relevant image is the so-called "Eternal Gospel" upon which Jung comments in *Answer to Job* as follows:

The first angel proclaims an "everlasting gospel," the
quintessence of which is "Fear God!" There is no more talk of God's
love. What is feared can only be something fearful.[1]

And then Jung enlarges upon the theme:

> Could anyone in his right senses deny that John correctly foresaw at
> least some of the possible dangers which threaten our world in the
> final phase of the Christian aeon? He knew, also, that the fire in which
> the devil is tormented burns in the divine pleroma for ever. God has a
> terrible double aspect: a sea of grace is met by a seething lake of fire,
> and the light of love glows with a fierce dark heat of which it is said
> "ardet non lucet"—it burns but gives no light. That is the eternal, as
> distinct from the temporal, gospel: *one can love God but must fear him*
> [italics Jung's].[2]

Understood psychologically, these comments refer to the fact that
proximity to the Self is accompanied by anxiety. Recall John's
response to the deity at the beginning of his vision in chapter one:
"When I saw him, I fell at his feet as though dead" (1:17). This dead
faint is a uniform feature in the Bible when individuals encounter
an angel or manifestation of the Lord; therefore, the very first
thing the angel must say is, "Fear not!" It is quite important to
understand this transpersonal dimension of anxiety. The experience of anxiety is not adequately dealt with personalistically—at
least not for adults—for whom anxiety often indicates nearness to
the Self. Indeed, every major anxiety experience is a kind of miniature "Apocalypse." At the outset of this book, I announced what I
consider to be the essential psychological meaning of the
Apocalypse: the coming into consciousness of the Self—and anxiety is a harbinger of that phenomenon. "One can love God but
must fear him."

ETERNAL TORTURE

This, then, brings up the theme of "eternal torture" as we find it
expressed in Revelation:

A third angel followed, shouting aloud, "All those who worship the beast and his statue, or have had themselves branded on the hand or forehead, will be made to drink the wine of God's fury which is ready, undiluted, in his cup of retribution; in fire and brimstone they will be tortured in the presence of the holy angels and the Lamb and the smoke of their torture will rise for ever and ever. There will be no respite, night or day, for those who worship the beast or its statue or accept branding with its name." (14:9–11) (See figure 7.1.)

I think we can state, in simplest terms, that "eternal torture by fire" refers to the fate of one who is wholly identified with the primordial psyche. When the Self is activated in an individual who is identified with the "Beast" (with the primordial psyche in its "Leviathan-Behemoth" combination) then that person will be "tortured" by compulsive desires for pleasure and power. Pleasure (hungry yearnings, envies, hatreds, everything pertaining to pleasurable gratification) and power (having to be superior, power gratifications of all sorts) are in fact the two great beastly principles. They are what alchemical texts refer to as the "crude sulfur"—as opposed to the true Sulfur.

It is Jung again who provides us with the classic description of the matter in *Mysterium Coniunctionis*, a passage worth reading and reflecting upon again and again because it is just filled with meaning. In the paragraph, Jung is speaking of an alchemical allegory as if he were interpreting a dream. And since it is a dream which any of us could have, the commentary applies to us all. Having connected a reference to "crude sulfur" with desirousness, he writes:

You too are infected with this collective sickness. Therefore bethink you for once . . . and consider: What is behind all this desirousness? A thirsting for the eternal, which as you see can never be satisfied with the best because it is "Hades" in whose honour the desirous "go mad and rave." The more you cling to that which all the world desires, the more you are Everyman, who has not yet discovered himself and stumbles through the world like a blind man leading the blind with somnambulistic certainty into the ditch. Everyman is always a multitude. Cleanse your interest of that collective sulfur which clings to all like a leprosy. For desire only burns in order to burn itself out, and in and

FIGURE 7.1

The Limbourg Brothers. *Hell,* from *Les Très Riches Heures du Duc de Berry.*
1413–1416. Illumination. Musée Condé, Chantilly, France.

from this fire arises the true living spirit which generates life according to its own laws . . . . This means burning in your own fire and not being like a comet or flashing beacon, showing others the right way but not knowing it yourself.[3]

Jung says more, but this is how one should understand psychologically the torturing fire in Revelation. It is the fire of *calcinatio* with all the symbolism that kind of operation implies.

But the question remains: Why is the "fire" of identifying with the primordial psyche eternal? Since this does not sound very auspicious for transformation, it must be understood in the context of the general nature of Christian scriptures, namely, as documents of *separatio*. As we shall see, Revelation does end with the image of wholeness—the "New Jerusalem" as a mandala city—but the contents of the book mainly involve a decisive, radical "separation" between heaven and earth, all things upper and lower, between spirit and matter or nature. This is a crucial feature of the Christian myth as it evolved and generated Western civilization out of itself, and it is a crucial feature of the Western psyche as a whole. We are all split. And within the myth, all that could be envisioned for an ending to the cosmic story was a permanent, eternal split. Although Origen in the third century could still consider the possibility of the redemption of the Devil, the idea could not be tolerated in Christianity—and Origen was branded a heretic. The Book of Revelation belongs to what we are calling the old aeon as a *separatio* document. It is a state of affairs, however, that is due to change in the new aeon. The coming "psychological aeon" is aiming towards the union of what has been split.

HARVESTING

Let us now consider the theme of "harvesting" as found in the following long apocalyptic passage:

Now in my vision I saw a white cloud and, sitting on it, one like a son of man with a gold crown on his head and a sharp sickle in his hand.

Then another angel came out of the sanctuary, and shouted at the top of his voice to the one sitting on the cloud, "Ply your sickle and reap: harvest time has come and the harvest of the earth is ripe." Then the one sitting on the cloud set his sickle to work on the earth, and the harvest of earth was reaped.

Another angel, who also carried a sharp sickle, came out of the temple in heaven, and the angel in charge of the fire left the altar and shouted at the top of his voice to the one with the sharp sickle, "Put your sickle in, and harvest the bunches from the vine of the earth; all its grapes are ripe." So the angel set his sickle to work on the earth and harvested the whole vintage of the earth and put it into a huge winepress, the winepress of God's anger, outside the city, where it was trodden until the blood that came out of the winepress was up to the horses' bridles as far away as sixteen hundred furlongs. (14:14–20) (See the sickle in God's hand in figure 6.4 above.)

What a terrible image! Although not spelled out explicitly, the underlying idea here is that humanity is a vast "agricultural process" for God to harvest for his own food and drink. The idea comes up elsewhere; it appears, for instance, in the seventh chapter of the apocryphal Old Testament scripture, 1 Enoch. There, Enoch is describing what was taking place just before Noah's flood, when angels or heavenly beings descended from heaven and married the daughters of men. Here is what he says:

And all the others together with them took unto themselves wives, and each chose for himself one, and they began to go in unto them and defile themselves with them, and they taught them charms and enchantments, and the cutting of roots, and made them acquainted with plants. And they became pregnant, and they bare great giants, whose height was three thousand ells: Who consumed all the acquisitions of men. And when men could no longer sustain them, the giants turned against them and devoured mankind. (7:1–4).[4]

Jung comments upon this passage in *Answer to Job* and says that the "giants" are pointing to "an inflation of the cultural consciousness at that period," just before the mythological Flood.[5] And I have published a dream with the same theme in *The Creation of Consciousness* which I will abbreviate here. But let me note first that I wish to demonstrate decisively by way of this significant apocalyptic dream that what we are dealing with in this entire book is not a set of abstract ideas and merely interesting imagery but *living psychic reality* that belongs to the here and now:

> I am walking along what appears to be the Palisades, overlooking all of New York City. . . . NYC is in a rubble—the world in fact has been destroyed as we know it. All of NYC is just one heap of rubble, there are fires everywhere, thousands of people are running in every direction frantically, the Hudson River has overflowed many areas of the city, smoke is billowing up everywhere. As far as I can see the land has been levelled. It was twilight; fireballs are in the sky, heading for the earth. It was the end of the world, total destruction of everything that man and his civilization had built up.
>
> The cause of this great destruction was a race of great giants—giants who had come from outer space—from the far reaches of the universe. In the middle of the rubble I could see two of them sitting; they were casually scooping up people by the handful and eating them. All this was done with the same nonchalance that we have when we sit down at the table and eat grapes by the handful. . . . the giants landed in flying saucers (the fireballs were other landings). In fact the earth as we know it was conceived by this race of giants in the beginning of time. They cultivated our civilization, like we cultivate vegetables in a hot house. The earth was their hot house, so to speak, and now they have returned to reap the fruits they had sown. . . . [6]

This modern dream and the texts of 1 Enoch and the Book of Revelation present imagery that is exactly parallel—because the meaning is as applicable today as it was in the ancient past.

What does it mean to be "eaten by giants?" It means to succumb to inflation, a psychological condition that is endemic in our time. In an interesting passage in the Gnostic Gospel of Thomas, Jesus says: "Blessed is the lion which becomes man when consumed by man; and cursed is the man whom the lion consumes, and the lion becomes man" (Logion 7).[7] Here are stated two possibilities: the first is that man eats lion, and lion becomes man; the second is that lion eats man, and man is assimilated to lion stuff—and blessed is one and accursed is the other. That is precisely the psychological issue for consciousness when the collective unconscious is activated or even when it lives itself through us unconsciously. To the extent that the ego is eaten by one of the archetypal "giants" or "lions," the human being has become inhuman; and that is a disaster. On the other hand, to the extent that the experience of the collective unconscious can be *assimilated* and understood by consciousness, then the archetypes are humanized. This is the issue behind the "harvesting" imagery in Revelation. And it is the fundamental issue running throughout all levels of existence: Who eats whom? It is absolutely elementary for all life processes and applies not only to the physical world but to psychological existence as well.

SEVEN GOLDEN BOWLS OF PLAGUES

We now turn to chapters 15 and 16 where we learn of the "seven bowls of plagues":

> After this, in my vision, the sanctuary, the tent of the Testimony, opened in heaven, and out came the seven angels with the seven plagues, wearing pure white linen, fastened around their waists with belts of gold. One of the four living creatures gave the seven angels seven golden bowls filled with the anger of God who lives for ever and ever. The smoke from the glory and the power of God filled the temple so that no one could go into it until the seven plagues of the seven angels were completed.
>
> Then I heard a voice from the sanctuary calling to the seven angels, "Go, and empty the seven bowls of God's anger over the earth." (15:5-8; 16:1) (See figure 7.2.)

Then, one after another, these seven bowls of plague and divine rage were emptied onto the earth. It is quite remarkable that these loathsome contents should be contained in "golden bowls." In a later chapter of Revelation, a golden cup appears in the hand of the Harlot who rides the Beast—another startling contrast between the feature of precious "gold" and the vessel's contents. As far as empir-

FIGURE 7.2

Dragons Vomiting Frogs. 15th century, C.E. Miniature from the *Liber Floridus.* Musée Condé, Chantilly.

ical psychology is concerned, a "golden bowl" represents the Self in its containing aspect with "gold" in particular representing supreme value. And that symbolism was explicit in alchemy. Thus, a devastating "plague" carried in a "golden bowl" is a paradoxical combination of opposites.

If we separate ourselves from the horror that this imagery evokes emotionally—and look at it momentarily in an objective and clinical way—we observe again that heaven is being cleansed of a lot of disagreeable stuff, which is then turned over to the earth to deal with. Psychologically, this is an image of very negative contents in the collective unconscious ("heaven") being poured into the ego ("earth"): and that indicates that there has been a build-up of disagreeable contents in the unconscious which has led finally to an "overflow." I think it is often relevant to consider psychological issues in this fashion—as if they were almost mechanical—in order to complement the tendency to project "punitive purpose" on the unconscious, something that is done frequently in the Book of Revelation. Ordinarily, however, the unconscious does not have a punitive purpose; instead, the unconscious tends to react to the ego the way that the ego reacts to it. And if the unconscious is used as a "depository" for everything disagreeable from the ego's point of view—as is so commonly the case—then sooner or later that depository will overflow! If we think in this mechanical way (in the way that we think of the law of gravity, even though it is not the whole story) we correct our tendency to interpret in overly-punitive terms.

It follows, then, that a psychological "overflow" can arise after a prolonged and profound neglect of the unconscious which has allowed the build-up of problematic libido the ego has disposed of by way of repression. In Judeo-Christian mythology, this same dynamic is put personally as the neglect of God's prerogatives, as failure to pay him the attention he is due—for which one then is punished. But I would say that the failure is worse than a "sin": it is a mistake, a psychological mistake. Putting it that way has the advantage of being more objective; and it does not demoralize one with a sense of guilt. It is hard enough for us to accept the mistakes that we have made, especially the big ones; and so a more conscious way of putting the matter is helpful.

Concerning the imagery of "plagues" descending from heaven, a modern dream has come to my attention:

> I am just above a heavy cloud cover, the way one is in an airplane. . . . The sky, the air, above the clouds is clear and blue. At first, it is like a movie, but I am really present as if at a theater performance. But it is in the open air, not in a theater. Directly opposite me, in the middle distance, is the Capitol dome, Washington, D.C. I think at first it is the real thing, then wonder if it isn't a stage set mock-up. It is illuminated, outlined, by many small lights, like the small lights at Christmas. . . . In the space between me and the Capitol dome comes a figure (an actor?) dressed as an angel. It says, "I've cut my hand." And a stream of blood is directed down to earth—AIDS-infected blood. (Immediately on awaking I think of the Prologue in heaven in Job and then also in *Faust*. I know, either in the dream or upon waking, that this means a plague of some sort.)

As the reader may know, some fundamentalist Christian ministers are offering a mythological interpretation of the modern plague of AIDS. According to them, the epidemic is caused by God's "anger" at sinful sexual misbehavior. But if we apply my principle—"It is more than a sin, it is a mistake"—the question arises with regard to AIDS and in response to this dream: What is the psychological mistake that causes AIDS?

There is profound symbolism involved in the phenomenology of the AIDS virus. And I suggest that the mistake which causes AIDS—speaking on the symbolic level—is a failure to "guard the borders" of one's individual identity. AIDS first appeared in what are euphemistically called "sexually active" male homosexuals. Some of these individuals are almost unbelievably promiscuous: I have heard from my own patients of repeated one-night stands with absolute strangers night after night, allowing unknown persons into their homes and into their bodies and into their psyches—with no sense of individual boundary. This is an exceedingly dangerous thing to do, on the physical level alone, inviting robbery and even murder. Psychologically, it is just as dangerous. Yet, these individuals feel so profoundly empty within themselves, that there arises a compulsion to be filled with some kind of intimate contact.

Compulsions, however, do not work; they are unconscious behaviors and merely repeat themselves. Sexual promiscuity is the sort of behavior that reveals a grave defect in the "boundaries" of individual identity. These boundaries are lacking, or they are porous, and the psychological doors are wide open.

Consider now the symbolism of the AIDS virus. The virus attacks and destroys the immune system specifically; that is its target. And the immune system is the physiological agent that protects the individual integrity of the organism. Whenever matter enters the blood stream, it is the immune system that asks: "Is this I or is it not-I? Does it belong to the identity of this organism or is it alien?" If the matter is alien, then the immune system destroys it; if not, the substance is accepted. But the AIDS virus attacks this protective agent by sneaking into its cells and directing the cells to make more of the virus—destroying the immune system cells from within. I think it is clear that the physiological operation of the virus is a picture of the psychological mistake that opened the door to the virus in the first place.

Here is another dream with a reference to AIDS—along with apocalyptic imagery—that Hill reports in *Dreaming the End of the World:*

> I'm visiting the friend of a gay man I know in a hospital in Florence, Italy. He is a Catholic priest dying of AIDS. My friend tells me before I meet the priest that his nose and mouth are rotten, so that I won't react with shock when I see him. I assure him that these things don't disturb me as I am a nurse—but inwardly I am uncertain.
>
> I tell the priest a dream about ecological disaster; and, as I do, I look out the window at Florence and see the cathedral in the center crumbling and the town itself falling to pieces into little islands and clumps of trees that scatter with the wind over the water.
>
> I climb up a rock escarpment and find refuge there. My cousins have also found higher ground nearby.[8]

We know only that the dreamer is a self-described "fallen Catholic," a personal fact that is immensely relevant to the picture of a "cathedral in the center crumbling." And it is important when working with dreams to work one's way downward, starting with the personal

reference and then on down to the collective or archetypal. But
Jung provides us with various examples of dreams in which
"churches are in ruins" signifying that we are dealing here not just
with a personal disaster but with a collective one: the falling apart of
the conventional, traditional, religious or mythological container of
our culture.[9] Not only does the priest who is rotting from AIDS
(mirrored by the church which is crumbling) point to the
Apocalypse, so does the dream image of "ecological disaster."

It may seem tangential, but the question of AIDS belongs to
the symbolism of organ transplants in modern medicine. I personally am against organ transplants—but then so is the immune system against them. The immune system will not accept organ
transplants and must be killed to keep a transplant intact. I side
with the immune system, however, because it is connected to the
unconscious.

FROGS

The Book of Revelation presents us next with the image of "frogs."
They appear in the sixteenth chapter where the "bowls of God's
anger" are being emptied over the earth:

> The sixth angel emptied his bowl over the great river Euphrates; all
> the water dried up so that a way was made for the kings of the East to
> come in [from Parthia, the dangerous enemy at that time]. Then from
> the jaws of dragon and beast and false prophet I saw three foul spirits
> come; they looked like frogs and in fact were demon spirits, able to
> work miracles, going out to all the kings of the world to call them
> together for the war of the Great Day of God the Almighty. (16:12–14)
> (See figure 7.2 above.)

It is not uncommon to come upon references to frogs in analytic
work. And even Nietzsche was obsessed with the idea that he should
somehow "swallow a toad"—as he was disturbingly informed by a
dream. Jung comments on that obsession in the *Zarathustra* semi-
nars as follows: "it is the expression of the loathsomeness of life, or
of the lower man"—"the inferior man living in the swamp or

mire."[10] Indeed, this was Nietzsche's problem; he was trying to live above his inferiority, his shadow. But frogs and toads are also, Jung observes, "the first attempt of nature towards making something like a man . . . so they are symbols for human transformation." And they reveal transformative qualities by metamorphosing from water-born tadpoles to amphibian adults. We think of the fairy tale of the "Frog Prince" which is a transformation tale: what began as a lowly frog—when accepted—became a prince.

Our image in the Book of Revelation, however, is the opposite of Nietzsche's obsession. Instead of being swallowed, frogs are being regurgitated: the direction is reversed as is the relationship to that lowly animal. In this regard, Hill records a most interesting apocalyptic dream:

> I'm in the desert near Alamogordo, New Mexico [where the first atomic tests were held]. Opening the door of a small ramshackle house with a tin roof, I see my father. His face is radiant, soft with pure sweet benevolence and he carries a poise very different from the drunken dissipation of when he was actually alive. He tells me, "It is time" and directs me to the door. I'm puzzled and excited—not knowing what I'm excited about.
>
> I climb on my rusty bicycle and rush down a slight slope to the desert below. The whole horizon is visible, and under the darkening skies the lights of the city flash on and off. The air is charged as if lightning will soon strike. I realize the Bomb is about to drop, and I race, ecstatic, toward Ground Zero so that I can meet it fully. In my waking life, I've never felt such ecstasy.
>
> At "Ground Zero" there is thunder without lightning. Instead of the Bomb, an odd frog-like creature drops out of the sky—floating down as slow as a feather, using its large webbed feet as wings. It's about three feet tall.
>
> As soon as it lands, it is attacked by local people. They beat it mercilessly. I intervene just as they are about to douse it with gasoline and light it.
>
> I sit with it and read it a children's book, trying to teach it English. It is very wise, but most of its wisdom seems in its capacity to play. It darts in and out of rabbit holes. I find myself frustrated even though I know that somehow the specialness of its intelligence is bound up with its playfulness—like a child's.[11]

This is a remarkable dream with much meaning. Although we have no personal information about the dreamer, we can observe that the dream-ego has a very different attitude toward the "frog" than is pictured in Revelation. True, the Christian attitude is also present in the dream—the local people try to exterminate the animal with fire—evidence of an emotional conflict going on within the dreamer about this issue. But the dream-ego does just the right thing and finds that in accepting this slimy animal associated with swamp and plague and demon spirits (finds in going the way of individuation) that the "frog-like creature" is a bringer of wisdom.

8 Revelation: Chapters 17, 18

THE WHORE OF BABYLON

We read at the beginning of chapter seventeen of Revelation:

> One of the seven angels that had the seven bowls came to speak to me, and said, "Come here and I will show you the punishment of the great prostitute who is enthroned beside abundant waters, with whom all the kings of the earth have prostituted themselves, and who has made all the population of the world drunk with the wine of her adultery." He took me in spirit to a desert, and there I saw a woman riding a scarlet beast which had seven heads and ten horns and had blasphemous titles written all over it. The woman was dressed in purple and scarlet, and glittered with gold and jewels and pearls, and she was holding a gold wine cup filled with the disgusting filth of her fornication; on her forehead was written a name, a cryptic name: "Babylon the Great, the mother of all the prostitutes and all the filthy practices on the earth." (17:1–5)

What a nasty image this is. At the outset, I think we can state that we have here a degraded version of "Venus." This is a perverted image of her and of ancient nature religion in general (see figure 8.1).

To see Venus differently portrayed, we have only to read the Roman poet and philosopher Lucretius (d. 55 B.C.E.) who dedicated to her his work, *On the Nature of Things*, in a period when Rome had not yet fallen into decadence but was living out of its older healthy religion. Lucretius writes about this divine mother of Aeneas who founded Rome:

133

FIGURE 8.1

William Blake. *Whore of Babylon.* Watercolor. British museum, London.

Mother of Rome, delight of Gods and men,
Dear Venus that beneath the gliding stars
Makest to teem the many-voyaged main
And fruitful lands—for all of living things
Through thee alone are evermore conceived,
Through thee are risen to visit the great sun—
Before thee, Goddess, and thy coming on,
Flee stormy wind and massy cloud away,
For thee the daedal Earth bears scented flowers,
For thee the waters of the unvexed deep
Smile, and the hollows of the serene sky
Glow with diffused radiance for thee!
For soon as comes the springtime face of day,
And procreant gales blow from the West unbarred,
First fowls of air, smit to the heart by thee.
Foretoken thy approach, O thou Divine,
And leap the wild herds round the happy fields
Or swim the bounding torrents. . . . .
Through leafy homes of birds and greening plains,
Kindling the lure of love in every breast,
Thou bringest the eternal generations forth . . . (1:1–25)[1]

Venus, as we can see, was once a carrier of sacred life energies; that
is what she meant to ancient healthy Rome. Of course, this image
did degenerate later in the imperial period.

What the image in Revelation shows us, however, is that everything "feminine" (earth, nature, body, matter) underwent a profound depreciation with the onset of our aeon. This was not
exclusively a matter of Christianity; because Stoicism and Platonism
did the same thing, if a bit more subtly, and even started the
process. Hellenistic and Christian Gnosticism was even worse in this
regard. I must caution the reader—since we live in a different age
with different values coming to birth—that everything that happens
in the psyche happens for an adequate reason. There is in philosophy the "principle of sufficient reason" which I think is particularly
applicable to psychological facts since it is so easy for the ego to take
the superficial attitude that certain psychological events in the

collective psyche were just errors and could have been different. They could *not* have been different—they had to be the way they were, given the nature of psychic reality. It is psychologically juvenile, therefore, to criticize some event in the collective psyche as though we know better how something should have happened. The fact is that the "depreciation of the feminine" is one of the ways by which the Western psyche has evolved; and we can only assume that it was necessary for the required sequence of events.

I agree with Jung that the vast, collective, individuation process which lies behind history required at the beginning of our era the creation of a powerful "spiritual" counterpole to the "instinctual" degradation and excesses that accompanied the decadence of the ancient world. What happened historically was a grand *sublimatio* operation prescribed by the collective psyche or collective unconscious at that time—a vast collective movement to get above the purely concrete, particular, bodily, material level of existence. That is the meaning of *sublimatio:* getting "above" it all, being able to "look down" on something. Indeed, if an individual is caught in the agony of suffering matter, it is no small achievement to gain a "spiritual" standpoint outside and above it. With regard to the historical dynamic, Jung says: "We can hardly realize the whirlwinds of brutality and unchained libido that roared through the streets of imperial Rome."[2] And this actual concrete state of affairs called forth in reaction the depreciation of all that carried the symbolic sign of the "feminine"—matter, body, and all those elements that chain us to suffering flesh.

The Golden Cup

Earlier, when we were speaking about the plagues that were poured out on mankind from heavenly bowls, I noted that these bowls were golden in spite of the nature of their contents. And here again we have what is called the harlot's "disgusting filth" contained in a "gold wine cup": a paradox, considering the many positive symbolic associations to gold that we have already observed. In my view, such paradoxes indicate the basic authenticity of these visions. There is no question that the original material has been conflated with a lot of Old Testament imagery which has been interwoven with the visions. But visions do not carry footnotes with them, they are spontaneous occasions. And so we can assume that the scriptural references were added subsequent to the experience. As Jung emphasizes, the outstanding proof of original content is the image of the "Sun-Moon Woman," but then so are the paradoxes in Revelation. We need only ask ourselves: "Supposing I have a dream of a golden cup or were brought in analysis a dream of a golden cup, how would I understand it?" Whatever its context, almost always it will symbolize the containing aspect of the Self, the Self in its feminine containing mode.

A fascinating history is attached to this image of the harlot's golden cup; it is a marvelous example of how the autonomous psyche works through the centuries, enlarging and elaborating and transforming itself as it goes along. Alchemy picked up this image of the "golden cup of Babylon" most specifically in Ripley's *Cantilena* which Jung discusses in detail and at length in *Mysterium Coniunctionis*.[3] In outline, the *Cantilena* is an alchemical parable about a barren old king who calls himself the "Ancient of Days." He complains about his sterile, barren state, and seeks rebirth or rejuvenation by returning to his mother's womb; he crawls right back into his mother's womb. As he goes, he states: "I'le Humbled be into my Mother's Breast,/Dissolve to my First Matter, and there rest (vs. 12)." The mother—who is now pregnant with this new conception—retires to her chamber, according to the parable. And here is the relevant stanza as she is in her chamber awaiting coming to term:

> Meanwhile she of the Peacocks Flesh did Eate
> And Dranke the Greene-Lyons Blood with that fine Meate,
> Which Mercurie, bearing the Dart of Passion,
> Brought in a Golden Cupp of Babilon. (vs. 17)

So the queen-mother, who is in the process of giving rebirth to the barren king, eats what Jung calls her "pregnancy diet"—consisting of peacock's flesh and lion's blood—served to her in the golden cup of Babylon, the very same cup that is such a prominent feature of the harlot in the Apocalypse of John.

This text has quite profound implications, because it announces (right on the face of it, if we just pay attention) the death and rebirth of the God-image. We are witnessing here the alchemical symbolic foreshadowing of the task of modern persons to reconcile the split opposites that exist in the Apocalypse—and in the Christian psyche—and *assimilate* consciously what is called the "disgusting filth of her fornication." Let me repeat, because it is so important: this obscure alchemical text is symbolically foreshadowing the modern task of assimilating all those contents that have been relegated to the shadow and thus have been considered despicable in the Christian dissociation. Since the peacock is the bird of the goddess Juno, Jung says that the "food of the Queen Mother—peacock's flesh and lion's blood—consists of the goddess's own attributes, that is to say she eats and drinks herself."[4] He then goes on to explain:

> she is being ruthlessly regaled with her own psychic substances. These are animal substances she has to integrate . . . peacock and lion with their positive and negative qualities; and the draught is given to her in the cup of fornication, which emphasizes still more the erotic nature of the lion, his lust and greed. Such an integration amounts to a widening of consciousness through profound insight.
>
> But why should such an unpalatable diet be prescribed for the queen? Obviously because the old king lacked something, on which account he grew senile: the dark, chthonic aspect of nature. And not only this but the sense that all creation was in the image of God, the antique feeling for nature [that Lucretius expressed so clearly above], which in the Middle Ages was considered a false track and an aberration. Dark and unfathomable as the earth is, its theriomorphic symbols do not have only a reductive meaning, but one that is prospective and spiritual. They are paradoxical, pointing upwards and downwards at the same time. If contents like these are integrated in the queen, it means that her consciousness is widened in both directions. This diet will naturally benefit the regeneration of the king by supplying what was lacking before. Contrary to appearances, this is not only the darkness of the animal sphere, but rather a spiritual nature or a natural

spirit which even has its analogies with the mystery of faith as the alchemists were never tired of emphasizing.[5]

Jung is describing here a process which now engages the collective psyche. The collective psyche is "eating peacock's flesh and drinking lion's blood" or—in terms of the imagery of Revelation—it is eating the "disgusting filth of her fornication." And some of it is pretty filthy, we have to admit, when we witness what is happening in the collective psyche as a whole as the old system of values collapses. All that has been excluded rushes back in. The onslaughts of violence, crude sexuality and wild orgiastic behavior, and disorientation of all kinds are symptoms of the process of assimilating contents which—nevertheless—are in a "golden cup." In other words, the value of the Self lies behind them: one can only hope not to be destroyed before reaching it.

THE WICKED CITY

The text of Revelation specifically states that the harlot is "Babylon the Great." Overtly, then, the harlot associates to the ancient city of Babylon; but, due to a number of allusions (such as the seven hills of Rome) and due to the author's living at the time of the Roman Empire, many commentators give priority to the harlot's association with the city of Rome. And there are some who believe that she refers to an apostate Jerusalem. As to the more obvious solution, we have an explicit reference in the Book of Jeremiah where Babylon had just defeated Israel and the city of Jerusalem and sent its inhabitants into captivity. Thus, Jeremiah prophesies:

> Yahweh says this:
> Against Babylon and the inhabitants of Leb-Kamai
> I shall rouse a destructive wind.
> I shall send winnowers to Babylon to winnow her
> and leave her country bare,
> for she will be beleaguered on all sides,
> on the day of disaster.

Let no archer bend his bow!
Let no man swagger in his breastplate!
—No quarter for her young men!
Curse her whole army with destruction!
In the country of the Chaldaeans the slaughtered will fall,
in the streets of Babylon, those run through by the sword. . . .

Babylon was a golden cup in Yahweh's hand,
she made the whole world drunk,
the nations drank her wine
and then went mad. (51:1–7)

As the reader can observe, some of these very phrases are incorporated in John's vision; and there is no question that the New Testament image looks back first of all to Babylon as a sort of prototypical evil city. Of course, Babylon had been long destroyed by the time of Revelation and did not require a prophecy of its downfall. Yet the image of "Babylon" as the evil city had been deposited in the Judeo-Christian psyche (see figure 8.2).

The chief reference to the city of Jerusalem as harlot can be found in the Book of Ezekiel:

The word of Yahweh was addressed to me as follows, "Son of man, confront Jerusalem with her loathsome practices! Say, 'The Lord Yahweh says this: . . . . I saw you kicking on the ground in your blood as I was passing, and I said to you as you lay in your blood: Live! and I made you grow like the grass of the fields. You developed, you grew, you reached marriageable age. Your breasts became firm and your hair grew richly, but you were stark naked. Then I saw you as I was passing. Your time had come, the time for love. I spread my cloak over you and covered your nakedness; I gave you my oath, I made a covenant with you—declares the Lord Yahweh—and you became mine . . .

But you became infatuated with your own beauty and used your fame to play the whore, lavishing your debauchery on all comers. You took some of your clothes to make for yourself high places bright with colours and there you played the whore. . . . And in all your loathsome practices and your whorings you never called your early days to mind, when you were stark naked, kicking on the ground in your own blood. (16:1–22)

FIGURE 8.2

Destruction of Babylon, from the *Cloisters Apocalypse.* ca. 1310–1320. Illumination. The Cloisters Collection, Metropolitan Museum of Art, New York.

On the basis of that imagery some scholars consider that the reference to an evil city in the Book of Revelation is to a backsliding Jerusalem that murdered the prophets Yahweh sent to her—a city, therefore, subject to God's wrath.

Still, the majority opinion holds that the city of Rome is meant by the author John, on the very adequate grounds that Rome did intermittently persecute the Christians viciously. And just as we have witnessed with other images in the Apocalypse, there have been later attributions as well. Early Protestants identified the harlot with the Catholic Church. And, interestingly, some contemporary fundamentalists have identified her with the ecumenical movement among Christian denominations as a traitorous, idolatrous violation of the one true message. Symbolically, of course, the "harlotry" of which Jerusalem is accused is idolatry or false worship in defiance of the one truth.

Psychologically, we are dealing here with the archetype of the "Wicked City." And at the very end of Revelation, we will be treated to the contrasting archetype of Jerusalem as the "Heavenly City" of Jerusalem. A universal image is involved, however, and the manifest city could just as well be—speaking phenomenologically—New York City. I am reminded of the fact that in his description of the decline of the West, Spengler speaks of the rise of the megalopolises as a symptom of decadence; the archetype of the Evil City, therefore, is subtly embedded in his speculations.

The "City" Archetype

To understand the matter more deeply, let us take up the image of the "city" by itself, without characterizing it. It is really an archetypal image that belongs to the symbolism of the mandala. Jung discusses that fact in *Psychology and Alchemy* where the theme of the city comes up in a dream series he is analyzing; he cites a Gnostic text that identifies the "city" with the metaphysical Monad or "One" which as first principle contains all things. The Coptic text reads: "This same is the Mother-City of the Only-begotten."[6] Conveniently, Jung has provided the Greek equivalent, *metropolis*, for "Mother-City" to help us see that the "city"—as a containing entity—is symbolically feminine; when the city is wicked, its personification will also be feminine. Something similar can be said of the "cup," which as container is symbolically feminine and open to personification. Jung writes:

> As "metropolis" the Monad is feminine, like the *padma* or lotus, the basic form of the Lamaic mandala . . . . In the Book of Revelation, we find the Lamb in the centre of the Heavenly Jerusalem. And in our Coptic text we are told that Setheus [the Monad as "creator"] dwells in the innermost and holiest recesses of the Pleroma, a city with four gates (equivalent to the Hindu City of Brahma on the world-mountain Meru).[7]

It follows that the "city"—as an inner image appearing in dreams—represents the Self as an ordered, structured totality. Scholars inform us that one of the early ways of founding a city was to plow a circular furrow all the way around the area to be enclosed and then to divide the circle into quarters. Construction would rise, then, from that basic mandala design. The city is a *temenos* or "sacred precinct."

Yet let us not forget that the city is also a literal external entity. It is the seat of civilization, as we know from the fact that the Latin word *civitas* is the root of both English words, "city" and "civilization." And that is because civilization comes only from life in cities. When we have an image such as this that we can recognize as an image of the Self—not just in individual psychology but living itself out externally as well—then we can observe the archetype at work, so to speak, in another medium. Of course, today the organized unit of civil or social life is no longer the city or *polis,* as in antiquity. Now, it is the nation-state. Thus, we have to think of the symbolism of the "city" in the context of the nation-state as a whole. But this means that as a concrete, external reality, the "city" of the nation-state is the collective, political mirror-image of the Self. And that is what gives nationalism its religious power. It is also true that when the archetype of the Self is collectively experienced as residing in the nation-state, that state will arrogate to itself the transpersonal authority that really belongs to the Self. Only a little experience of dealing with government bureaucracy will demonstrate that fact.

To a much lesser degree, we could say the same thing about the Church. It likewise is the earthly, collective embodiment of the Self. In modern times, however, the Church has been so enervated that it is less dangerous than the state, having no physical power at its disposal. That, of course, was not always the case; and in earlier times the Church, too, arrogated to itself the transpersonal authority that really belongs to the Self.

Augustine made considerable use of "city" imagery in the early fifth century C.E. In his major work, *The City of God,* he spoke of two cities: an "Earthly city" and a "Heavenly city" which he also called the "city of God." The Earthly city was thought to be made up of individuals who lived by love of self—self with a small "s" as in ordinary selfishness; by contrast, the "city of God" was made up of individuals living by the love of God. The first was typified by Babylon, says Augustine; while the second was typified by the Heavenly Jerusalem whose image we find at the end of the Book of Revelation. Now, Augustine did not make the crude mistake of identifying the city of God concretely with the Christian Church as some theologians subsequently were tempted to do. He even stated that membership in the Church did not necessarily grant one membership in the City of God. In other words, Augustine's "Heavenly city" was not a literal entity but an image on a spiritual level. This, then, allows us to understand the same imagery of *The City of God* in a psychological way: namely, that the "Earthly city" is the *ego,* and the "City of God" is the *Self.* Both are "cities," and both are built on the same ground plan; but the ego is built on the ground plan of the Self. As Jung tells us explicitly, the Self is a prefiguration of the ego.[8]

Much later than Augustine, the German philosopher Hegel was also gripped by the archetypal image of the "City." In his grand vision of the historical process, he saw the "World Spirit" operating in human history in both individuals and institutions; and, as of 1820, he saw its highest manifestation to be the organic, cultured community of the nation-state. This was in Hegel's view the earthly incarnation of God. It was not, as his critics still claim, a crude glorification of the Prussian state; but Hegel's manner of speaking does lay him open to that criticism. Actually, he was a remarkable figure gripped by the archetypal image of the "City" as the Self. And he projected that image into the sophisticated notion of an ideal nation-state community: in which individual rights and freedom would exist within the framework of a community of transpersonal awareness that carried objective supra-personal purposes and values.[9]

I mention this because the collective psyche does indeed operate in this way. The Self is projected into one's national community and is the basis of national and ethnic identity. This psychology, for instance, lies behind the conflict between Israelis and Palestinians over the city of Jerusalem—but also between the north and south of Ireland, between religious and secular Muslims. Collective exteriorized manifestations of the Self lead inevitably to the constellation of the opposites contained in the Self; and those opposites generate conflict. The latent "conflict of opposites" in the God-image then lives itself out in the drama of human history: opposing groups go to war. And the individuals involved are the helpless pawns of the archetypal images that possess them!

9 Revelation: Chapters 19, 20

THE LAST JUDGMENT

These chapters bring to our attention one great image, that of the "Last Judgment," which we will now explore at some length. John writes:

> Then I saw a great white throne and the One who was sitting on it. In his presence, earth and sky vanished, leaving no trace. I saw the dead, great and small alike, standing in front of his throne while the books lay open. And another book was opened, which is the book of life, and the dead were judged from what was written in the books, as their deeds deserved. (20:11–12)

Here we have in visionary form a central tenet of the Christian creed. It appeared first as a formula embedded within the so-called Apostles' Creed of the fourth century where we find the essential contents of the Christian myth. Here is a standard version of that creedal statement as found in the Anglican *Book of Common Prayer* (1945):

> I believe in God the Father Almighty, Maker of heaven and earth:
> And in Jesus Christ his only Son our Lord: Who was conceived by the Holy Ghost, Born of the Virgin Mary: Suffered under Pontius Pilate, Was crucified, dead, and buried: He descended into hell; The third day he rose again from the dead: He ascended into heaven, And sitteth on the right hand of God the Father Almighty: From thence he shall come to judge the quick and the dead.

> I believe in the Holy Ghost: The Holy Catholic Church: The
> Communion of Saints: The Forgiveness of sins: The Resurrection of
> the body: And the Life everlasting. Amen.[1]

Not only is the notion of a "Last Judgment" an integral part of the
Creed, it is an immensely important archetypal image in all the
major religions. Typically, the world's religions postpone the event
as long as possible, at least until the "afterlife"—while Christianity
delays it as long as possible, projecting it into the "end of the aeon."
But the effect of the postponement is always the same: namely, to
spare the individual the experience of "Judgment" in his own lifetime.[2] When one observes that phenomenon so consistently, one
can be sure there is good reason for it—a final objective judgment
is, indeed, a fearsome thing to contemplate. S.G.F. Brandon has
written a very good book on this subject, *The Judgment of the Dead,*
gathering much of the relevant material from the world's religions;
but, as with so many good books in a culture such as ours, it is out
of print.[3] Brandon presents data from ancient Egypt and
Mesopotamia, the Hebrew religion, Greco-Roman culture,
Christianity, Islam, Persian religion, Hinduism, Buddhism, and the
religions of China and Japan—just to give some sense of the widespread archetypal nature of this theme. I will have to limit my references, however, to the Bible, Greco-Roman culture, and Egypt;
but it should be obvious that when the image of "judgment" comes
up in analysis, there is more than enough material available for
amplification.

The evidence is quite clear that one phenomenological aspect
of the *activated* Self is the generation of the ego experience of being
judged: 1) as to how it is living its life; 2) and with regard to the psychological attitude with which that ego is living. I am putting the
matter in this twofold way in order to include not only the ego's
actual deeds but also the psychological facts that lie behind those
deeds—we all know, of course, that outer actions do not always
reveal the true psychology of an individual. As I have said, however,
the anticipation of being judged in these ways has been so frightening that historically the experience has been projected as far away
as possible. Nevertheless, the time has come for depth psychology

to understand that this great image of the "Last Judgment" is a psychological experience available while one is alive and conscious. It is the experience of a decisive encounter with the Self that requires specifically a thorough assimilation of the shadow. We know this is the requirement since Last Judgment imagery consistently concerns shadow issues.

A particularly outstanding reference to the "Last Judgment" in the Old Testament is found in Malachi where Yahweh proclaims:

> Look, I shall send my messenger to clear a way before me. And suddenly the Lord whom you seek will come to his Temple; yes, the angel of the covenant, for whom you long, is on his way, says Yahweh Sabaoth. Who will be able to resist the day of his coming? Who will remain standing when he appears? For he will be like a refiner's fire, like fullers' alkali. He will take his seat as refiner and purifier; he will purify the sons of Levi and refine them like gold and silver, so that they can make the offering to Yahweh with uprightness. The offering of Judah and Jerusalem will then be acceptable to Yahweh as in former days, as in the years of old. I am coming to put you on trial and I shall be a ready witness against sorcerers, adulterers, perjurers, and against those who oppress the wage-earner, the widow and the orphan, and who rob the foreigner of his rights and do not respect me, says Yahweh Sabaoth. (3:1–5)

Should the reader ever question that these texts have been edited and redacted in order to mitigate their emotional impact, consider this final phrase from the Jerusalem Bible version: "no need for you to be afraid of me, says Yahweh"! Incidentally, Handel uses this very scripture in his fourth aria of "The Messiah" where we hear: "The Lord will suddenly enter his temple. Who will be able to resist the day of his coming? Who will remain standing when he appears? For he is like the refiner's fire."[4]

The New Testament uses various terms for the image of the Last Judgment. It is called, for example, the "Day of Judgment" or the "Last Day" and also the "Coming" (a translation of the Greek *parousia* which literally means "presence"). According to the Christian Creed, Christ's sojourn on earth was followed by his death, then his ascension into heaven, and finally by his return to earth—specifically for the purpose of Judgment. This image of the "Coming" of Christ merges with the image of the coming of the "Kingdom of God" or "Kingdom of Heaven," as overlapping motifs signifying similar material. Concerning the Last Judgment, the Gospel of Matthew provides the key description:

> When the Son of Man comes in his glory, escorted by all the angels, then he will take his seat on his throne of glory. All nations will be assembled before him and he will separate people one from another as the shepherd separates sheep from goats. He will place the sheep on his right hand and the goats on his left. Then the King will say to those on his right hand, "Come, you whom my Father has blessed, take as your heritage the kingdom prepared for you since the foundation of the world. For I was hungry and you gave me food, I was thirsty and you gave me drink, I was a stranger and you made me welcome, lacking clothes and you clothed me, sick and you visited me, in prison and you came to see me." Then the upright will say to him in reply, "Lord, when did we see you hungry and feed you, or thirsty and give you drink? When did we see you a stranger and make you welcome, lacking clothes and clothe you? When did we find you sick or in prison and go to see you?" And the King will answer, "In truth I tell you, in so far as you did this to one of the least of these brothers of mine, you did it to me." Then he will say to those on his left hand, "Go away from me, with your curse upon you, to the eternal fire prepared for the devil and his angels. For I was hungry and you never gave me food, I was thirsty and you never gave me anything to drink, I was a stranger and you never made me welcome, lacking clothes and you never clothed me, sick and in prison and you never visited me." Then it will be their turn to ask, "Lord, when did we see you hungry or thirsty, a stranger or lacking clothes, sick or in prison, and did not come to your help?" Then he will answer, "In truth I tell you, in so far as you neglected to do this to one of the least of these, you neglected to do it to me." And they will go away to eternal punishment, and the upright to eternal life. (25:31–46)

This scripture puts matters rather starkly, but it was the basis for all medieval representations of the Last Judgment, culminating in Michelangelo's magnificent fresco on the back wall of the Sistine

Chapel. There we find the returning Christ as a kind of "traffic director"—one stream of beings sent heavenward, and the other stream directed down to hell. Now, I think it is of interest that virtually all truly medieval versions of the Last Judgment have a clear-cut boundary line between heaven and hell, a definitive break in reliefs and paintings between upper and lower registers. That is not the case, however, in Michelangelo's picture—which I take to be a symptom of the Renaissance when the dissociation between "upper and lower" in the psyche begins to break down (see figure 9.1).

The Matthew text is particularly important psychologically because it establishes the fact that the "Greater" personality (the Self) is found in the "least" of psychological manifestations. In other words, those aspects of the psyche that the ego despises and which are most likely to be neglected are precisely where the Self resides: "In truth I tell you, in so far as you neglected to do this to one of the least of these, you neglected to do it to me." This is, of course, a kind of paradox, that the personality in its transpersonal greater form should be manifest in the least. But it makes very good sense psychologically; because the process of coming into awareness of one's wholeness involves the acceptance and assimilation of all those shadow aspects that one has previously considered the most despicable. The way to the Self is through the "least" aspects of ourselves, a theme I have previously touched upon in a case history found in *The Living Psyche*.[5]

JUDGMENT IN GREECE AND ROME

As I have stated, the notion of a "Last Judgment" is by no means an invention of Judeo-Christian mythology. For instance, a judgment after death is pictured in a Platonic myth found in the tenth book of *The Republic*. Socrates is discussing the issue of justice during and after life and tells the story of a warrior named Er who had been slain in battle and left for dead. When his corpse was brought home, he suddenly revived—to recount what he "had seen in the world beyond" during his apparent death experience:

FIGURE 9.1

Michelangelo. *The Last Judgment* (detail). 1534–1541. The Sistine Chapel, Rome.

He said that when his soul went forth from his body he journeyed with a great company and that they came to a mysterious region where there were two openings side by side in the earth, and above and over against them in the heaven two others, and that judges were sitting between these, and that after every judgment they bade the righteous journey to the right and upward through the heaven with tokens attached to them in front of the judgment passed upon them, and the unjust to take the road to the left and downward, they too wearing behind signs of all that had befallen them, and that when he himself drew near [to be judged also] they told him that he must be the messenger to mankind to tell them of that other world, and they charged him to give ear and to observe everything in the place. (10.614)[6]

The story continues. But I wish to call attention to the following detail as the two types of departed souls report their experiences: "the one lamenting and wailing as they recalled how many and how dreadful things they had suffered and seen in their journey beneath the earth—it lasted a thousand years—while those from heaven related their delights and visions of a beauty beyond words." Here we witness the motif of the "millennium" or a thousand years in association with judgment. That, too, has not been invented by the Christian Book of Revelation but has been plucked right out of Plato.

There is another important example from the Greco-Roman period in Plato's *Gorgias*. Again, Socrates is speaking:

Give ear then, as they say, to a very fine story, which you, I suppose, will consider fiction, but I consider fact, for what I am going to tell you I shall recount as the actual truth. As Homer says, Zeus and Poseidon and Pluto divided their kingdom among themselves after inheriting it from their father. Now in the days of Cronus there was this law about mankind, which from then till now has prevailed among the gods, that the man who has led a godly and righteous life departs after death to the Isles of the Blessed and there lives in all happiness exempt from ill, but the godless and unrighteous man departs to the prison of vengeance and punishment which they call Tartarus. And in the days of Cronus and even when Zeus was but lately come to power, living men rendered judgment on the living, pronouncing sentence on the very day on which these were to die, and so the verdicts were not well given. Accordingly, Pluto and the stewards from the Isles of the Blessed came and told Zeus that the wrong people were going to both places. Then Zeus said, "Well, I will put a stop to that. Cases are judged badly now," said he, "because those who are tried come to judgment with their clothes on, for they are still alive when judged. And therefore many," said he, "who possessed evil souls are invested with fine bodies and linage and wealth, and when the trial takes place, many witnesses come forward to testify that they have lived righteous lives. So the judges are dazzled by these, and at the same time they are clothed themselves when they give sentence, their eyes, their ears, and their whole bodies acting as a screen before their souls. They have all these hindrances before them, both their own clothing and that of those on trial. First of all then," said he, "men must be stopped from foreknowing their deaths, for now they have knowledge beforehand. . . . Next they must be stripped naked of all these things before trial, for they must be judged after death. And the judge must be naked too and dead, scanning with his soul itself the souls of all immediately after death, deprived of all his kinsmen and with all that fine attire of his left on earth, that his verdict may be just. Now I had realized all this before you, and I have appointed sons of mine as judges, two from Asia, Minos and Rhadamanthus, and one, Aeacus, from Europe. And when these are dead, they will hold court in the meadow, at the crossroads from which two paths lead, one to the Isles of the Blessed, the other to Tartarus. And Rhadamanthus will judge those who come from Asia, Aeacus those from Europe, and to Minos I will grant the privileges of court of appeal, if the other two are in doubt, so that the judgment about which path men take may be as just as possible." (523–24)[7]

This is very interesting material, because it reveals countless years of folk wisdom reflecting on the archetype of the "Last Judgment"— here crystallized out in a particular legend.

It is significant that Zeus has ordered the Last Judgment to be done in conditions of both "deadness" and "nakedness." I believe these conditions, psychologically considered, are related. The reader may recall that Jung described his own near-death experience as a painful "stripping away" of everything except his very essence.[8] In other words, the dying process itself is a stripping to nakedness: the condition of deadness and the condition of nakedness are symbolically analogous. We are reminded also of the alchemical pictures in the *Rosarium Philosophorum* where the process of *conjunctio* begins with the King and Queen clothed; but, as they proceed to wholeness, they must be stripped of their clothing and left with the "naked truth"—as Jung puts it—of what they represent.[9] Christ says, "Do not judge, and you will not be judged" (Matthew 7:1). But we must judge and be judged as part of psychic existence; still, it should be done in a state of what the *Rosarium* calls *mortificatio* and in the "nakedness" of the ego. It is not really surprising that these experiential images of death and nakedness accompany the encounter with the Apocalypse archetype since the archetype includes exposure to the unerring "eye of God" which sees us as we really are. It follows that the experience requires the conscious assimilation of the shadow.

We find another classic example of this phenomenon in the sixth book of the *Aeneid*. During his trip to the underworld, Aeneas is told about judgment in the afterworld. Here is Dryden's translation:

> These are the realms of unrelenting Fate;
> And awful Rhadamanthus rules the state;
> He hears and judges each committed crime;
> Inquires into the manner, place, and time.
> The conscious wretch must all his acts reveal
> (Both to confess, unable to conceal),
> From the first moment of his vital breath,
> To his last hour of unrepeating death,
> Straight o'er the guilty ghost, the Fury shakes
> The sounding whip, and brandishes her snakes,
> And the pale sinner, with her sisters, takes. (6.763–773)[10]

The Virgilian image of the Furies' snaky whips appears in Michelangelo's "Last Judgment" scene.

JUDGMENT IN ANCIENT EGYPT

Working our way backward, we arrive at ancient Egypt and at what was probably the very earliest manifestation of the Last Judgment archetype. It goes back at least five thousand years. According to the *Larousse Encyclopedia of Mythology*, an Egyptian who died had to go through a series of ordeals, including what the Greeks called *psychostasia* or "weighing the soul" of the dead:

> When the deceased had, thanks to the talismans placed on his mummy and especially to the passwords written on the indispensable Book of the Dead with which he was furnished, safely crossed the terrifying stretch of country between the land of the living and the kingdom of the dead, he was immediately ushered into the presence of his sovereign judge, either by Anubis or by Horus. After he had kissed the threshold he penetrated into the "Hall of Double Justice." This was an immense room at the end of which sat Osiris . . . . redeemer and judge who awaited his "son who came from earth." In the centre was erected a vast scale beside which stood Maat, goddess of truth and justice, ready to weigh the heart of the deceased. Meanwhile Amemait, "the Devourer"—a hybrid monster, part lion, part hippopotamus, part crocodile—crouched nearby, waiting to devour the hearts of the guilty. All around the hall, to the right and to the left of Osirus, sat forty-two personages. . . . forty-two judges, each corresponding to a province of Egypt; and each was charged with the duty of examining some special aspect of the deceased's conscience.
>
> The deceased himself began the proceedings and without hesitation recited what has been called "the negative confession" [an extended list of all the sins the soul claims not to have committed].[11] (See figure 9.2.)

What follows is the "weighing" of this soul. In one of the pans of the balance, the goddess Maat herself is represented by a feather as the symbol of Truth—while in the other pan rests the heart of the deceased. The scales are carefully read, the result written down; and if the two pans of the balance are in perfect equilibrium, then Osiris renders a favorable judgment, saying: "Let the deceased depart victorious. Let him go wherever he wishes to mingle freely with the gods and the spirits of the dead." Thus, the dead one was justified and lead into a life of eternal happiness in the kingdom of Osiris. But if the pans did not balance, the heart—which contained the soul or which was the soul—was fed to the waiting monster: it went

FIGURE 9.2

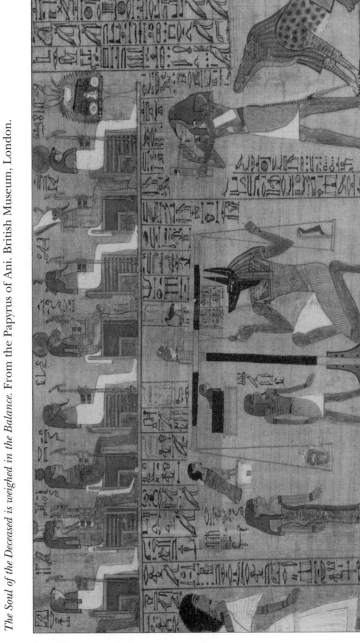

The Soul of the Deceased is weighed in the Balance. From the Papyrus of Ani. British Museum, London.

into the maw of hell. One can see that this imagery antedates by many thousands of years the same imagery in the Book of Revelation.[12]

THE BALANCE

Let us explore this image of the "balance" a bit more as it occurs in the fifth chapter of Daniel. The Babylonian king Belshazzar was giving a great feast when suddenly there appeared on the palace wall handwriting which no one in the hall could interpret. Daniel—an Israelite in exile who was nevertheless renowned for his "perception, intelligence and wisdom comparable to that of the gods"—was called; and this is what he had to say:

> The writing reads: *mene, mene, teqel,* and *parsin.* The meaning of the words is this: *mene:* God has *measured* your sovereignty and put an end to it; *teqel:* you have been *weighed* in the balance and found wanting; *parsin:* your kingdom has been *divided* and given to the Medes and the Persians. (5:25–28)

And that same night Belshazzar was murdered. Now, philologists have understandably expended a great deal of effort trying to determine the source of the three words: *mene, teqel,* and *parsin.* And with reasonable certainty the word *mene* does mean "to measure"; the word *teqel* means "to weigh out" and the word *parsin* "to divide." So, "measure, weigh, and divide" are the three basic terms which the prophet Daniel elaborated, saying in effect: "It's your sovereignty that has been measured, and a limit has been put on it; it's you who has been weighed in the balance and found wanting; and your kingdom is going to be divided, broken up." The terms are relevant because they are part of the phenomenology of the Last Judgment archetype.

As recently as the nineteenth century, Ralph Waldo Emerson wrote of the archetypal image of the "balance" in a beautiful way that demonstrates his profound intuition into the nature of things. The following passage comes from his essay on "Compensation":

A wise man will extend this lesson to all parts of life, and know that it is the part of prudence to face every claimant and pay every just demand on your time, your talents, or your heart. Always pay; for first or last you must pay your entire debt. Persons and events may stand for a time between you and justice, but it is only a postponement. You must pay at last your own debt. If you are wise you will dread a prosperity which only loads you with more. Benefit is the end of nature. But for every benefit which you receive, a tax is levied. He is great who confers the most benefits. He is base—and that is the one base thing in the universe—to receive favors and render none. In the order of nature we cannot render benefits to those from whom we receive them, or only seldom. But the benefit we receive must be rendered again, line for line, deed for deed, cent for cent, to somebody. Beware of too much good staying in your hand. It will fast corrupt and worm worms. Pay it away quickly in some sort.[13]

And all of this is said as an explication of the principle:

The terror of cloudless noon, the emerald of Polycrates, the awe of prosperity, the instinct which leads every generous soul to impose on itself the tasks of a noble asceticism and vicarious virtue are the tremblings of the balance of justice through the heart and mind of man.[13]

This same "balance of justice" is what our society's current personification of blind "Justice" holds in her hands. And it associates to being level, straight, fair, honest—balanced. It is, psychologically put, an aspect of the activated Self which imposes its objective standard on the ego. I do not believe one ever escapes it. I suspect that those persons who have totally disregarded this principle of "compensation" all of their lives have the experience at the time of their death; at least, that is what the mythological sources suggest.

Practically all this material—the reader may have noticed—concludes with a more or less decisive "split afterlife": a separation between the sheep and the goats, between the blessed and the condemned, between the upper and the lower realms. That imagery points to a dissociation in the collective psyche. But I think that depth psychology has discovered the basis for healing that split, reconciling those split opposites in the totality of the Self—eventually, if not in the near future. The most important factor is that depth psychology has transferred this crucial experience of "Judgment" in an afterlife to the psyche, to the inner world of the living individual. It can now be seen as potentially a conscious experience during one's life here on earth; and in this way the psychological view transcends much of the traditional Christian imagery.

Jung describes one version of such an experience in *Memories, Dreams, Reflections* where he speaks of an encounter with the Self—which has "arrived" in an irreconcilable conflict of duties. As long as one has a clear sense of duty in a given situation, there is some moral guidance as to how one should proceed. But supposing one is confronted with two irreconcilable duties of equal weight simultaneously: What then? Here is what Jung says:

> But if a man faced with a conflict of duties undertakes to deal with them absolutely on his own responsibility, and before a judge who sits in judgment on him day and night, he may well find himself in an isolated position. There is now an authentic secret in his life which cannot be discussed—if only because he is involved in an endless inner trial in which he is his own counsel and ruthless examiner, and no secular or spiritual judge can restore his easy sleep. If he were not already sick to death of the decisions of such judges, he would never have found himself in a conflict. For such a conflict always presupposes a higher sense of responsibility. It is this very quality which keeps its possessor from accepting the decision of a collectivity. In his case the court is transposed to the inner world where the verdict is pronounced behind closed doors.
>
> Once this happens, the psyche of the individual acquires heightened importance. It is not only the seat of his well-known and socially defined ego; it is also the instrument for measuring what it is worth in and for itself ["measure," let us recall, is embedded in Belshazzar's word *mene*]. Nothing so promotes the growth of consciousness as this inner confrontation of opposites. Quite unsuspected facts turn up in the indictment, and the defense is obliged to discover arguments hitherto unknown. In the course of this, a considerable portion of the outer world reaches the inner, and by that very fact the outer world is impoverished or relieved. On the other hand, the inner world has gained that much weight by being raised to the rank of a tribunal for ethical decisions. However, the once unequivocal ego loses the pre-

rogative of being merely the prosecutor; it must also learn the role of defendant. The ego becomes ambivalent and ambiguous and is caught between hammer and anvil. *It becomes aware of a polarity superordinate to itself* [italics Jung's].[14]

That polarity superordinate to the ego is the Self. But I wish to repeat something Jung has just said: "In the course of this, a considerable portion of the outer world reaches the inner, and by that very fact the outer world is impoverished or relieved. On the other hand, the inner world has gained that much weight by being raised to the rank of a tribunal for ethical decisions." That is precisely the process we are engaging here by interpreting scriptures in a psychological way. Prior to now, these texts have been enshrined as dogma in the collective psyche and, therefore, have been part of the outer world. By understanding the psychological reality that stands behind them, we are "impoverishing" the scriptures of their content or "relieving" them of the weight of their content (Jung makes use of both words which carry different nuances) while at the same time augmenting the weight and magnitude of the psyche. That operation is going on in this book.

10 Revelation: Chapters 21, 22

THE NEW JERUSALEM

The Book of Revelation ends with a grand finale, with a great mandala and *coniunctio* vision. The mandala is the "New Jerusalem" which an angel shows to John. In ecstasy, John writes:

> In the spirit, he carried me to the top of a very high mountain, and showed me Jerusalem, the holy city, coming down out of heaven from God. It had all the glory of God and glittered like some precious jewel of crystal-clear diamond. The wall was of a great height and had twelve gates; at each of the twelve gates there was an angel, and over the gates were written the names of the twelve tribes of Israel; on the east there were three gates, on the north three gates, on the south three gates, and on the west three gates. The city walls stood on twelve foundation stones, each one of which bore the name of one of the twelve apostles of the Lamb. . . .
>
> The plan of the city is perfectly square, its length the same as its breadth. . . . and equal in height [the city is actually a cube]. The wall was built of diamond, and the city of pure gold, like clear glass. The foundations of the city wall were faced with all kinds of precious stone: the first with diamond, the second lapis lazuli, the third turquoise, the fourth crystal, the fifth agate, the sixth ruby, the seventh gold quartz, the eight malachite, the nine topaz, the tenth emerald, the eleventh sapphire, and the twelfth amethyst. The twelve gates were twelve pearls, each gate being made of a single pearl, and the main street of the city was pure gold, transparent as glass. I could not see any temple in the city since the Lord God Almighty and the Lamb were themselves

the temple, and the city did not need the sun or the moon for light, since it was lit by the radiant glory of the God, and the Lamb was a lighted torch for it. . . . and there will be no night there . . . . Nothing unclean may come into it: no one who does what is loathsome or false, but only those who are listed in the Lamb's book of life.

Then the angel showed me the river of life, rising from the throne of God and of the Lamb and flowing crystal-clear. Down the middle of the city street, on either bank of the river were the trees of life, which bear twelve crops of fruit in a year, one in each month, and the leaves of which are the cure for the nations. (21:10–27; 22:1–2)

This is a magnificent mandala image, a complex quaternity which is really a city of precious stone. It thus has, as Jung points out, many parallels with the alchemical lapis. Indeed, whenever one encounters dreams involving "precious stones," it is generally a reference to the Self which is eternal and beautiful (see figure 10.1).

This grand image also reproduces certain features of the original state of paradise with its river of life and the trees of life along its banks. It is, therefore, specifically a place of healing; for the leaves of these trees are the "cure" for all. I am reminded—by way of amplification—of Jung's dream, reported in *Memories, Dreams, Reflections,* which came three times in the spring and early summer of 1914 just prior to the First World War. In each dream, an intense Arctic cold descended over all of Europe. Yet, as Jung tells us:

In the third dream frightful cold had again descended from out of the cosmos. This dream, however, had an unexpected end. There stood a leaf-bearing tree, but without fruit (my tree of life, I thought), whose leaves had been transformed by the effects of the frost into sweet grapes full of healing juices. I plucked the grapes and gave them to a large, waiting crowd.[1]

This needs no interpretation; clearly the "tree of life" within the heavenly Jerusalem and within Jung's dream are related.

There is also in the grand finale of Revelation an image of *coniunctio,* a *hierosgamos* or "sacred marriage": the beautiful city is identified explicitly as "the bride that the Lamb has married" (21:9). Concerning this, Jung has made specific remarks in *Answer to Job:*

FIGURE 10.1

Gustave Doré. *The New Jerusalem* ca. 1866. Engraving.

This final vision, which is generally interpreted as referring to the relationship of Christ to his Church, has the meaning of a "uniting symbol" and is therefore a representation of perfection and wholeness:
hence the quaternity, which expresses itself in the city as a quadrangle,
in paradise as the four rivers . . . . While the circle signifies the round-
ness of heaven and the all-embracing nature of the "pneumatic" deity,
the square refers to the earth. Heaven is masculine, but the earth is
feminine. Therefore God has his throne in heaven, while Wisdom has
hers on the earth, as she says in Ecclesiasticus: "Likewise in the beloved
city he gave me rest, and in Jerusalem was my power." . . . The city is
Sophia, who was with God before time began, and at the end of time
will be reunited with God through the sacred marriage. As a feminine
being she coincides with the earth, from which, so a Church Father
tells us, Christ was born.[2]

While we learn here that the celestial City is not only the Bride but
also equivalent to Wisdom, there is a problem: the "marriage" takes
place in the pleroma, in the transcendent realm, rather than on the
earthly level. Despite the likelihood that this wonderful image was
meant to be of greatest universality, Jung was nevertheless obliged
to continue:

No doubt this is meant as a final solution of the terrible conflict of existence. The solution, however, as here presented, does not consist in
the reconciliation of the opposites, but in their final severance, by
which means those whose destiny it is to be saved can save themselves
by identifying with the bright pneumatic side of God.[3]

What we have here is a superimposition of two different levels of
symbolism. I have pointed out repeatedly in this work that the Book
of Revelation depicts a cosmic *separatio* process, a vast cosmic split
between "heaven and hell." But then there comes this ending—a
magnificent *coniunctio* and quaternity image implying a reconciliation of opposites, a state of wholeness. On the concrete level, it
appears that redactors have patched this final image onto the original which gives the scripture as it stands a strange double-layered
character. But the historical likelihood of that happening is not the

chief point. For it remains true that the collective psyche has generated this particular text, has used these redactors, and preserved the text as it appears. Psychologically, we must take the Book of Revelation as it has come to us. And I think that the meaning of this double-layered structure is this: at certain levels of development a decisive *separatio* is, in fact, a state of wholeness—even if not what we, with modern psyches, would define as a state of wholeness. Whenever one reaches a decisive developmental stage that fulfills the innate potential of *one's time* and *one's nature,* then images of the Self will signify "fulfillment." Looked at from the perspective of a later time and a later developmental stage, those same images can be seen to be in conflict with each other. I do not expect this point to be perfectly clear, however, since a paradox remains in the scripture.

THE MESSIANIC BANQUET

Traditionally, there should now occur in the story of Revelation a wedding feast since the "heavenly Jerusalem" is being married to the "divine Lamb." But this image is not explicit in Revelation. It is, however, explicit in Jewish legend as the "Messianic banquet" of which I have already spoken. In that great meal, the faithful ones are to be served the meat of Behemoth and Leviathan; and they are to drink wine made from grapes grown in paradise. This imagery does sneak into the nineteenth chapter of Revelation:

> I saw an angel standing in the sun, and he shouted aloud to all the birds that were flying high overhead in the sky, "Come here. Gather together at God's great feast. You will eat the flesh of kings, and the flesh of great generals and heroes, the flesh of horses and their riders and of all kinds of people, citizens and slaves, small and great alike." (19:17–18)

The flesh being offered is of those who will be slaughtered during the Apocalypse—a grisly version of the symbolic wedding feast, of course, but there it is. I have observed a parallel motif in a dream to which I have already referred and which was reported in my book, *The Creation of Consciousness*. The reader may recall that the dreamer, from the other side of the river, is observing New York City in a state of ruins. Giants from outer space have descended and are eating human beings: "They cultivated our civilization, like we cultivate vegetables in a hot house. The earth was their hot house, so to speak, and now they have returned to reap the fruits they have sown." The dream goes on, and we learn that the dreamer is going to be spared because he has slightly high blood pressure. Instead of being eaten, he must submit to an ordeal:

> We walked for an extraordinary long time, witnessing cataclysmic destruction. Then before me I saw a huge golden throne, it was as brilliant as the sun, impossible to view straight on. On the throne sat a king and a queen of the race of giants. They were the intelligences behind the destruction of our planet. . . .
>
> The ordeal or task I had to perform, in addition to witnessing the world's destruction, was to climb up this staircase until I was at their level—"face to face" with them. This was probably in stages. I started climbing, it was long and very difficult, my heart was pounding very hard. I felt frightened but knew I had to accomplish this task, the world and humanity were at stake. I woke up from this dream perspiring heavily.
>
> Later I realized that the destruction of the earth by the race of giants was a wedding feast for the newly united king and queen . . . .[4]

This image is very close to the one we have been examining in the Book of Revelation. And so we have to ask ourselves: How are we to understand psychologically this grisly wedding feast which has appeared in an ancient text and in a modern man's dream? This is what I suggest. The "Apocalypse"—and apocalyptic material of any sort from any age—signifies that the archetypal "opposites" which make up the God-image have been activated and have set off the dynamism of the *coniunctio* or the archetypal problem of "love and war." The opposites, of any sort, either unite in love or clash in enmity. When this *transpersonal* dynamism touches the conscious ego, it engages the *human* psyche, both individually and collectively. And it is then that the process insists on being "incarnated," so to speak—insists upon manifesting itself concretely, acting itself out unconsciously or otherwise. To do this, however, the archetypal dynamic must draft or conscript human beings into its service. Yet this means that human beings will be "consumed" or "devoured" by the process which then deprives them of their personal lives. Archetypal factors make them mere "actors" in the archetypal drama. And usually this drama lives itself out unconsciously, willy-nilly, in collective human history where *everyone* is a victim. The more conscious alternative is that an individual who understands what is going on "incarnates" the archetypal process as individuation.

In this context, I often think of an important sentence Jung just slips into *Answer to Job:* "the *imago Dei* pervades the whole human sphere and makes mankind its involuntary exponent. . . ." [5] Easily, a whole volume could be written on the implications of that one thought, and I have commented upon it already in my *Transformation of the God-Image.*[6] In brief, Jung's statement means that when the *imago Dei* is particularly activated, the God-image "eats" human beings; it does not just pervade them but possesses them and, in effect, "consumes" their egos. That explains the horrible aspect of the "wedding feast" in Revelation.

RESTORATION

Now, just prior to these materials, we read in chapter 21 of the Book of Revelation:

> Then I saw a new heaven and a new earth; the first heaven and the first earth had disappeared now, and there was no longer any sea. I saw the holy city, the new Jerusalem, coming down out of heaven from God, prepared as a bride dressed for her husband. Then I heard a loud voice call from the throne, "Look, here God lives among human beings. He will make his home among them; they will be his people, and he will be their God, God-with-them. He will wipe away all tears from their eyes; there will be no more death, and no more mourning or sadness or pain. The world of the past has gone.
> Then the One sitting on the throne spoke. "Look, I am making the whole of creation new." (21:1–5)

In addition to the clearly stated theme of incarnation here—"God-with-them"—there is in the passage the very important notion of *apocatastasis,* generally translated "restoration" and referring to the restitution of all things, a new heaven and earth, a new creation. While the actual word does not appear in Revelation, it is spoken by Peter in Acts of the Apostles where he says:

> "Now you must repent and turn to God, so that your sins may be wiped out, and so that the Lord may send the time of comfort. Then he will send you the Christ he has predestined, that is Jesus, whom heaven must keep till the universal restoration [*apocatastaseos panton,* literally, "restoration of all"] comes which God proclaimed, speaking through his holy prophets." (Acts 3:19–21)

The idea is that originally the world was perfect, whole, complete. But Adam sinned, we are told—psychologically, ego consciousness entered into the created world—spoiling the original state of whole-ness. At the appointed time, however, that original state of whole-ness is going to be restored: there is going to be an *apocatastasis,* a new creation, a new heaven and earth, corresponding to the origi-nal one but on a new level. This notion does not originate with Jewish and Christian literature but was generally active in the col-lective psyche of the ancient period. The Stoics, for example, imag-ined the universe to be an infinite series of cyclical cosmic periods in which the *apocatastasis* was the final stage of an old period and the beginning of a new one. But the image gains special prominence through the Christian writings of Origen in the third century. While posthumously declared a heretic, he was the most important Greek-speaking theologian of his time and spoke extensively on the *apoc-atastasis* to which a whole chapter in book one of *On First Principles* was dedicated. Here is an excerpt:

> The end of the world and the consummation will come when every soul shall be visited with the penalties due for its sins. This time, when everyone shall pay what he owes, is known to God alone. We believe, however, that the goodness of God through Christ will restore [bring about an *apocatastasis*] his entire creation to one end, even his enemies

being conquered and subdued. (I.6.1)[7]

In order to make his point, Origen cites various scriptures that refer to a time, sooner or later, when everything will be subject to God or Christ. And his point was that ultimately even the devil will be redeemed. This was a psychologically generous position unique among the Early Christian Fathers; and so I, for one, have a particular fondness for Origen. Of course, he had to be branded heretical by the Church—how could it have been otherwise? He had a sense of ultimate wholeness, beyond the split of the Christian aeon.

Psychologically, we can understand *apocatastasis* as the ego's restored relation to the Self after a long period of estrangement. The whole process of ego development—from infancy to maturity—involves an elaborate estrangement from the original complete relation to the Self which, nevertheless, had one rather sizeable defect: it was unconscious. The reader can explore this matter further in the first section of *Ego and Archetype* where I describe the ego as being born out of the Self, then going through various stages of inflation and alienation, eventually—provided the ego develops far enough—to return to a relation to the Self on a conscious level. This I believe is the psychological background of the grand image of a "restoration of all things" as it pertains to the Apocalypse archetype in the Book of Revelation.

FINAL THOUGHTS

In conclusion, it remains for me to address in a more general way what it means for modern persons to be living in an apocalyptic age. I think it is evident to perceptive people that the Apocalypse archetype is now highly activated in the collective psyche and is living itself out in human history. The archetypal dynamic has already started, is already moving among us. And, in that respect, the fundamentalists are right in their preoccupation with this particular imagery: the trouble is they are approaching the phenomenon anachronistically, with a psychology that was operative and appropriate two thousand years ago: with concretistic metaphysical projections. They really do expect to be caught up into the air in a literal rapture at the end of the age. Yet, there is no doubt from the *psychological* data that the Apocalypse is now living itself out in the collective psyche in an unconscious and, therefore, destructive way. The evidence is everywhere. The Self is coming, and the phenomena that ought to be *experienced consciously and integrated by the individual in the course of the individuation process* are occurring unconsciously and collectively in society as a whole. This fact is in accord with the psychological law that an activated psychic content not realized consciously manifests externally in the outer world. It is my conviction that we are at the threshold of a time of trouble of immense proportion. How massive the catastrophe will be will depend on how many individuals have achieved a sufficient level of individuation to know what is going on.

In this regard, I see Jung's great work, *Answer to Job,* as a crucial factor. On April 2nd, 1955, Jung wrote the following in a letter in which he was explaining why he had written that book:

> Just as Job lifted his voice so that everybody could hear him, I have come to the conclusion that I had better risk my skin and do my worst or best to shake the unconsciousness of my contemporaries rather than allow my laxity to let things drift towards the impending world catastrophe.[8]

I find this to be an astonishing statement. Jung was aware that he, one individual out of five billion, could perhaps avert or mitigate the impending world catastrophe by what he tells us in *Answer to Job*. And that is why he shares the information found there.

As I see it, *Answer to Job* is the one and only antidote the individual has while obliged to endure (and hopefully to survive) the ordeal of the Apocalypse in its collective manifestation. This one terse and passionate work tells us what is going on, the *meaning* of the vast collective upheaval of which we are now in the beginning stages: namely, that it is the coming of the Self into collective awareness, the "incarnation of the God-image" with all its paradoxical ambiguity, a God who unites within himself both good and evil. Jung spells that out explicitly in this short work, describing the profound divine drama that is unfolding in the collective psyche.

Actually, *Answer to Job* is part of a trilogy of works on the same topic: first, there is *Aion;* then *Answer to Job* which is the heart of the trilogy; and then *The Undiscovered Self*—which English title, incidentally, was chosen by the publishers while Jung preferred *Present and Future,* a title more clearly related to the apocalyptic experience. In each of these works, the essential idea is that the Self, the new God-image, *is* coming! It is visiting the earth, visiting humanity, visiting the individual ego: and it is coming in order to incarnate itself. "Yahweh" wants to become man again, more fully. And *Answer to Job* is the talisman to help us to get through the process.

Let us, then, listen to Jung:

> Yahweh's decision to become man is a symbol of the development that had to supervene when man becomes conscious of the sort of God-image he is confronted with. God acts out of the unconscious of man and forces him to harmonize and unite the opposing influences to which his mind is exposed from the unconscious. The unconscious wants both: to divide and to unite. In his striving for unity, therefore, man may always count on the help of a metaphysical advocate, as Job clearly recognized. The unconscious wants to flow into consciousness in order to reach the light, but at the same time it continually thwarts itself, because it would rather remain unconscious. That is to say, God wants to become man, but not quite. The conflict in his nature is so great that the incarnation can only be bought by an expiatory self-sacrifice offered up to the wrath of God's dark side.[9]

That "expiatory self-sacrifice" is the ordeal that humanity must now undergo as the untransformed God-image enters the human sphere in search of its own transformation. As I have said repeatedly, it is a psychological rule that if an activated psychic content is not integrated consciously, it will be manifest externally in a literal concrete way. Emerson recognized with his uncanny insight one aspect of this rule when he wrote in his first published essay, *Nature:*

> Every man's condition is a solution in hieroglyphic to those inquiries he would put. He acts it as life, before he apprehends it as truth.[10]

It follows that if we wish to know the nature of certain unrealized aspects of our psychology we have only to examine the circumstances that confront us. Our external condition is really a picture of those psychic entities not yet understood.

Conversely, we can also say that an inimical external event which is threatening to happen may be averted or mitigated by one's becoming conscious of its inner, psychic origin. If a danger can be experienced psychologically, one can often be spared the concrete experience of it; and generally the psychic experience is much more manageable. There are people, for instance, who dream of having car accidents: indeed, this may mean they are in grave danger of literally having car accidents—if what the "car accident" signifies is so unconscious that it has to stage an accident to get attention. And so, sometimes, the analyst must very earnestly warn the patient: "You're in danger of having a literal car accident!" The unconscious can be very stupid in this regard, getting its point across at whatever cost to the human being with whom it is trying to communicate.

These matters are relevant to our apocalyptic age. The "coming of the Self" is imminent; and the process of collective "individuation" is living itself out in human history. One way or another, the world is going to be made a single whole entity. But it will be unified either in mutual mass destruction or by means of mutual human consciousness. *If* a sufficient number of individuals can have the experience of the coming of the Self as an individual, inner experience, we may just possibly be spared the worst features of its external manifestation. I cannot state that possibility with certainty but merely as a hypothesis for which we do have, as already noted, some psychological data. Yet this is how we might lessen the dynamic urge in the collective psyche to manifest the "Apocalypse" collectively and concretely in its most extreme form.

When the Self comes, it necessarily brings the "opposites," since they are its essential content. As long as the Self is unconscious, however, these opposites lie side by side peacefully—the "lion lies down with the lamb"—because there is no consciousness of their distinction or separateness. But once this essential content touches the area of consciousness, the opposites split apart: and the individual ego is confronted with "conflict." Then, there arises the crucial question whether or not the ego is able to contain the conflict of opposites as a psychological problem to be met with consciousness. Unfortunately, that task is very difficult. Jung writes:

> All opposites are of God, therefore man must bend to this burden; and in so doing he finds that God in his "oppositeness" has taken possession of him, incarnated himself in him. He becomes a vessel filled with divine conflict.[11]

What usually happens is that the individual is not able to contain this "warring" within one's own self, and the conflict of opposites spills out into the outer world by way of projection. And it is then that the constellated opposites live themselves out not in the vessel of the individual psyche, but in the vessel of society as a whole. This is precisely what is happening today. The God-image is living out its oppositeness in the bitter factional disputes breaking out all over the world: at this writing, among warring clans in Somalia; between Tutsis and Hutus in Rawanda; Serbs and Bosnians in Yugoslavia; Palestinians and Israelis in the Middle East; not to mention our own fanatical political-action groups at war with each other on the American political scene. The list could go on and the names might change from year to year. But this troubling short list of "conflicts," which is so easy to compile, reminds us of Heraclitus's remark, "War is the father of all." These many factions are what Jung refers to as the wretched "isms"—and yet all are part of the phenomenology of the Apocalypse.

What are we to do? Let us listen again to Jung at length from *Answer to Job:*

> The only thing that really matters now is whether man can climb up to a higher moral level, to a higher plane of consciousness, in order to be equal to the superhuman powers which the fallen angels have played into his hands. But he can make no progress with himself unless he becomes very much better acquainted with his own nature. Unfortunately, a terrifying ignorance prevails in this respect, and an equally great aversion to increasing the knowledge of his intrinsic character. . . . We can, of course, hope for the undeserved grace of God, who hears our prayers. But God, who also does *not* hear our

prayers, wants to become man, and for that purpose he has chosen, through the Holy Ghost, the creaturely man filled with darkness—the natural man who is tainted with original sin and who learnt the divine arts and sciences from the fallen angels. The guilty man is eminently suitable and is therefore chosen to become the vessel for the continuing incarnation, not the guiltless one who holds aloof from the world and refuses to pay his tribute to life, for in him the dark God would find no room.

Since the Apocalypse we now know again that God is not only to be loved, but also to be feared. He fills us with evil as well as with good, otherwise he would not need to be feared; and because he wants to become man, the uniting of his antinomy must take place in man. This involves man in a new responsibility. He can no longer wriggle out of it on the plea of his littleness and nothingness, for the dark God has slipped the atom bomb and chemical weapons into his hands and given him the power to empty out the apocalyptic vials of wrath on his fellow creatures. Since he has been granted an almost godlike power, he can no longer remain blind and unconscious. He must know something of God's nature and of metaphysical processes if he is to understand himself and thereby achieve gnosis of the Divine.[12]

This ordeal of the Apocalypse—beginning now and to which all of humanity is being subjected—corresponds to Job's ordeal in the Bible yet even more pertinently to Christ's ordeal. Christ was the first attempt of the God-image to incarnate and transform itself. Now, the second time around, humanity as a whole and not just one person is going to be the subject of that process. God is going to incarnate in humanity as a whole and in that incarnated form offer himself as a self-sacrifice to bring about his own transformation—just as he did with the individual Christ. The matter is put clearly if densely by Jung in his classic letter to Elinid Kotschnig in June of 1956:

Christ . . . was up against an unpredictable and lawless God who would need a most drastic sacrifice to appease His wrath, viz. the slaughter of His own son. Curiously enough, as on the one hand his self-sacrifice means admission of the Father's amoral nature, he taught on the other hand a new image of God, namely that of a Loving Father in whom there is no darkness. This enormous antinomy needs some explanation. It needed the assertion that he was the Son of the Father, i.e., the incarnation of the Deity in man. As a consequence the sacrifice was a self-destruction of the amoral God, incarnated in a mortal body.[13]

This passage can be applied precisely to Yahweh's second act of incarnation in humanity as a whole. Humanity is now in the role of the "son of the God." And God is bringing about his own transformation by another self-destruction while incarnated in the "mortal body" of humankind. There will follow necessarily, archetypally, the same sequence of events as occurred in the life of a single individual but now in a larger arena. And this second act of incarnation likewise will bring about the same goal, a transformation of the God-image. The image of a totally good God—albeit pestered by a dissociated evil Satan—is no longer viable. Instead, the new God-image coming into conscious realization is that of a paradoxical union of opposites; and with it comes a healing of the metaphysical split that has characterized the entire Christian aeon.

This is what can happen potentially. But the process of transforming the God-image can take place only if its human participants are *conscious* of what is happening, because consciousness is the agency of transformation for God and man. There is, of course, no transformation of the God-image if we end up with nothing but a heap of ruins and a group of savages having to make the laborious climb to civilization all over again. But the God-image can incarnate in a way that averts massive destruction if there are enough individuals aware of the unfolding archetypal drama that is before us.

I do have to share with the reader that it is my view that the transformation of the God-image is ultimately certain: because one person, Jung, has already realized what is going on. I believe that is all it takes in principle to bring about eventually a positive outcome (but then, "eventually" can be a long time). My hypothesis remains, however, that the extent of the destructive collective process will depend on how many other individuals can achieve Jung's level of consciousness. How many will it take to reach this critical mass that will make a difference? The Book of Revelation hints at the number "144,000"—but what that symbolic number means literally cannot be known.

Let us return, somewhat more on a personal level, to Jung's comment in *Answer to Job* and ask what it means to say: "Since [humanity] has been granted an almost godlike power, he can no longer remain blind and unconscious. He must know something of God's nature and of metaphysical processes if he is to understand himself and thereby achieve gnosis of the Divine."[14] What does it mean to have an understanding of "metaphysical processes" and "gnosis of the Divine"? How can we apply such phrases to our own personal lives? I believe the answer is relevant to every depth analysis—that is, to analysis that actually goes into the "depths." Every depth analysis is a miniature "apocalypse": the individual experiences a conflict of opposites (of one kind or another), the frustration of their resolution, defeat, demoralization or despair—leading to an impairment or paralysis of libido flow (as if there were a "destruction of one's world" from which conscious "civilization" has to start all over again). All these experiences are standard symptomatic events prior to and during analysis. But if healing is to take place and life is to go on in fullness, the nature of the situation has to be understood. *Meaning* has to be found; the painful process itself must be found meaningful. And so these questions naturally arise in the analytic work: "What's happening here? Why does this happen to me? Where does the responsibility lie? And what does it mean?"

In the study of one's personal life history—going back through the traumas of early experience that make up so much of our personal complexes—shallow answers to these questions may be found. And if that method suffices to provide sufficient meaning that heals, so be it. But often it does not; and one must go deeper. It is then that one may come eventually to the Self, the paradoxical God-image that Jung discusses so fully in *Answer to Job*. The experiences one has in that encounter, the knowledge that one gains in the process, is what Jung means by "gnosis of the Divine." And when that is achieved, the neurosis is finally healed.

These same matters apply on a vast collective scale as humanity begins to experience world-wide apocalyptic events. The same questions arise: "Why is this happening? Who is responsible? What does it all mean?" And those questions take on increasing urgency the more desperate circumstances become. In contrast to the conscious process of individuation, the answers to these questions are dealt with collectively in large-scale regressive phenomena: the atavistic return to religious Fundamentalisms; the disintegration of complex social structures and reversion to more primitive social arrangements; massive collective shadow projections leading to factional wars and violence of all kinds on all social levels (from the family, to the neighborhood gang, and on up to the national level); and by widespread despair leading to increases in suicide and to addictions of all kinds. In general, there occurs a disintegration of social and psychic structures and values which have been the architecture of the collective psyche—no longer "contained" by an operative religious myth. And I see these tendencies as potentially being so widespread that they generate vast waves of psychic contagion tending to infect even those who might otherwise have sufficient consciousness to resist them. Vast collective psychic moods have immense contagious power.

I paint this terrible picture, as a backdrop, in order to repeat what I believe is a possible mitigating factor. In the midst of this horrendous state of affairs, it is just possible that Jung's message—as he presents it in *Answer to Job*—will finally gain the attention of enough members in society to draw his message into general view so that it will receive some discussion, at least, beyond the modest readership of this book. If that were to happen, people might then begin to get a glimmer of the meaning of the collective upheaval we are all having to endure. Perhaps a certain sufficient number of the creative minority would begin to entertain the idea that a vast historical "transformation of God" is going on and that the ordeal is the necessary "sacrificial" event to bring about that transformation. Putting it differently, as Jung does in *The Undiscovered Self:* "We are living in what the Greeks called the *kairos*—the right moment—for a 'metamorphosis of the gods', of the fundamental principles and symbols. This peculiarity of our time, which is certainly not of our conscious choosing, is the expression of the unconscious man within us who is changing."[15]

Finally, here are two dreams that I believe make many of these points symbolically. The first came to me from an adult while I was lecturing on the "Archetype of the Apocalypse":

The dreamer was in a room that was very white, light and larger than the real room that it referred to. And a white, fine ash, a powdery dust began to seep through the doors and windows even though the room was tightly closed. Someone said that considerable money had been spent sealing the room and expressed failure that the effort had failed. And I knew that the ash had come from an atomic bomb test in Nevada; and I felt frustrated at the government's resumption of testing and concerned about the well-being of myself, the cats, and others. We tried to sweep away the radioactive ash, but I worried that it had already contaminated everything. (On awakening, I felt a frightening loss of control.)

The second is from Hill's collection, dreamed by a ten-year-old girl, which I offer as a kind of amplification of the first to see if some meaning "shines" through their similarity:

The television and radio were buzzing and melting. A snake that slithered out of the television said, "The reason you are seeing all this is because it's the beginning of a nuclear war." It was a peace snake.

I started looking for the snake when the Bomb blew up. Me and a few other kids were the only ones left. There weren't any adults alive.

Me and my friends had to take the parts of broken-up houses and make a new shelter. When I was looking for wood, I found the peace snake, but it was dead. We dug a deep hole where we buried the snake, and we built our house over it.

At night, blue and silver and black and red dust blew in. We thought it was good dust, but it turned out to be radiation dust. It coated the house. A kid who had helped us build the shelter died. Later a few other kids died, too, so we had a small graveyard.

Sparkling white dust blew in the next night. We thought it was bad dust, too, but it wasn't. It flew into our house. There was a big pile of it near the hole where we buried the peace snake. We heard these murmuring words from the hole saying, "Put some of this white dust in the hole and you'll cure me. It's peace dust." So we did.

That night it grew into a beautiful big snake with all these different colors, and it curled around the whole house. It told us whenever there was going to be a radioactive storm.

A peace storm came that made the snake grow and covered the ground with white dust like thick snow. We found that, if we put a little peace dust on our plates, we'd have fruit and things to eat. And when it melted, it dissolved the radioactive dust with it.

After the peace dust went away, there was a big forest and a few houses and people. Different wild animals walked around and weren't afraid of people. There were no big buildings or apartments. The peace snake became our pet.[16]

There are several motifs in these dreams, but if we focus upon their common image of "white dust" produced by some atomic or nuclear explosion—which, as I have noted, is a common feature of modern apocalyptic dreams—then we witness in both instances the dream ego's attitude of resistance to its "arrival." In the adult's dream, however, the white radioactive ash is decidedly negative; while in the child's dream, its value is ambiguous—indeed, eventually the dangerous stuff in this second dream is called "peace dust." It really does matter how one interprets these matters depending on the personal age of the dreamer. The dreamer may be at a later stage of life when more shadow assimilation is required—in which case the coming of even more "whiteness" would have a negative implication, objectively.

But if we analyze generally, we can say that "dust" belongs to the alchemical symbolism of *sublimatio.* "White dust," then, is white "foliated" earth in alchemical terms: It is earth that has been pounded so intensely that it approaches the state of a gas—becoming smoky, vaporous stuff suspended in air. Psychologically, one is dealing with "earthy" entities (the "disgusting" earthy entities represented by the Whore of Babylon in the Book of Revelation) which have been subjected to real-life ordeals of one kind or another. When the imagery is specifically "ash," it is due to the alchemical ordeal of *calcinatio* which is a fiery spiritualizing process. But if we look again at both dreams, it is evident that the strange apocalyptic substance of "white dust"—whatever its meaning—*insists* on making its presence known. The dreams make it clear that one cannot hermetically seal oneself off from it; there is no escape. Indeed, "white radioactive ash" represents events outside the ego that require the conscious attitude of opening up to them, of accepting them in some way, if one is to survive.

I repeat the principle, one more time, that "Apocalypse" imagery for the *individual* signifies disaster only if the ego is alienated and antagonistic toward the realities that the Self is bringing into consciousness. It is then that the archetype of the Apocalypse must manifest catastrophically. But if the ego is open and co-operates with the "coming of the Self," the very same imagery can signify, as Jung puts it, a "broadening out of man to the whole man."[17]

The apocalyptic events depicted in the Book of Revelation are at hand. Jung's *Answer to Job,* if we can assimilate it, provides us with the *meaning* of these events. Certainly, Jung thought his understanding of these matters was worth his best efforts to communicate: "rather than allow [his] laxity to let things drift toward the impending world catastrophe."[18]

Appendix I
A Case History of Possesion by the Apocalypse Archetype: David Koresh

It seems to me that we need a new category by which to understand persons who are possessed by the Apocalypse archetype. They often exhibit features of the criminal and the madman, of course, and yet they are possessed by transpersonal, archetypal dynamisms which are inherently religious. Let us call them "zealots."[1] To demonstrate explicitly what it can mean for someone to be possessed in this way, I bring to your attention the life of Vernon Howell, also known as David Koresh. The reader may recall that in the spring of 1993, he was the central figure in the national and international news surrounding the small town of Waco, Texas: his apocalyptic sect was at war with Federal agents there. Approaching this person as a case history is difficult, however, since there is not much clinical information available—authors have other interests and one must gather bits and pieces by the way.[2] Yet we do know that Vernon Howell had a troubled childhood. He was born in 1959 of a fourteen-year-old mother whom he did not know until he was five. He was raised in his early years by an aunt and thought she was his mother until— one shocking day—the biological mother arrived and announced, "No, I'm your mother." Vernon's father was missing right from the start and never did appear. Keep in mind that when one misses certain vital childhood relationship experiences, it will mean that the individual has been deprived of the opportunity to incarnate or personalize those archetypes. A completely missing parent figure leaves a kind of "hole" in the psyche through which raw *unmediated* energies of the original archetype can flow; and we will see what that unmediated flow will do to Vernon. Later, there was on the family

183

scene a punitive step-father. At school, the boy seems to have exhibited a learning disability since he was taunted by the other children with "Retard, retard!" Older boys also sodomized him.

But then there was the grandmother. She belonged to the Seventh-Day Adventist Church—a fundamentalist denomination that emphasizes the imminent return or "advent" of Christ at the End of the world. It is essentially apocalyptic in its focus. And this grandmother took Vernon to church regularly from around the age of six. They had a good relationship; and the boy began to study the Bible intensely.

In Howell's late teens and early twenties, there came a period of Bunyanesque lostness. He suffered from a severe compulsion to masturbate accompanied by a profound sense of guilt—indicating that he experienced the Christian dissociation from sexual libido in a particularly marked form. He took on odd jobs. Then, something happened about which we have no information: Vernon Howell moved rather suddenly from a state of dissociation concerning power and sex drives to identification with them. He came into contact with a splinter group of Seventh-Day Adventists called Branch Davidians and inserted himself into their midst—gradually taking them over with very intelligent power-plays, knowing exactly what he was doing![3] And in the process of becoming the unquestioned charismatic leader of the group, he not only satisfied his power motive but gratified his sexual urges as well. He pronounced as his own wife—at the command of God—any woman in the group who caught his fancy, very young or simply unattached or already married to one of his loyal followers. This, one can readily see, is an entirely different state of affairs—psychologically—from that of the earlier state of a dissociated split accompanied by victim psychology and masturbation guilt. But the apparent "integration" of sex and power libido has been won by way of the ego's quasi-psychotic identification with the Self.

Howell developed a full-blown possession by the Apocalypse archetype. He was convinced that God had revealed to him total understanding of the Book of Revelation. In fact, he was engaged in writing a commentary on the "Seven Seals" when the armed agents of the Bureau of Alcohol, Tobacco, and Firearms invaded his compound; and he even agreed to surrender when he was finished with that work. But, then, Vernon Howell had already become identified with the "Apocalyptic Lamb." In 1985, he had a vision during a trip to Israel in which God told him he was none other than the reincarnation of Cyrus—the Persian king who had rescued the Israelites from Babylonian captivity: and so he changed his name to "David Koresh," David the archetypal king of Israel and Koresh meaning Cyrus in Hebrew. And so, he would write in a wedding invitation two years later words the reader will recognize from apocalyptic scripture:

> I have seven eyes and seven horns. My name is the Word of God and I ride on a white horse. I am here on earth to give you the seventh angel's message. I have ascended from the east with the seal of the living God. My name is Cyrus, and I am here to destroy Babylon.[4]

From that point on if not earlier, David Koresh cultivated his family of followers and required absolute obedience. He administered harsh punishment for even minor infringements of the rules and would fall into passionate rages when crossed—if criticized, he would react with a combination of personal intimidation and theological reasonings. There was always this bizarre combination of the personal and the transpersonal. But he had so mastered the Bible in his early comforting years with his grandmother (apparently that is what had kept him alive), that he was now capable of innumerable, interminable, crazy but brilliant Bible sermons—they could last all night. And always the message preached was that the "End of the world" was coming soon. We have here an illustration of a typical example of possession by the archetype of the Apocalypse. And if one is possessed by that archetype, it inevitably leads to catastrophe—because "catastrophe" is built into the archetypal pattern. The individual, so possessed, must make it happen in order to fulfill the archetype's structure. And that, tragically, is how Vernon Howell—a.k.a. David Koresh—came to his fiery death at the age of thirty-four.

   I believe that the study of such identifications with an archetype is valuable for understanding the psyche, since they reveal to us the nature of the *unrealized* Self. As I stated at the outset of this book, the Apocalypse archetype means essentially the "coming of the Self." Thus, to be possessed by that archetype means to be possessed by that process. But if the Self "arrives" in an unconscious or primordial form, the process manifests as a paradoxical combination of opposites: it is both savior and beast. Indeed, that is how David Koresh behaved, both at the same time; otherwise, we could not explain the loyalty of his followers. He was not psychotic by ordinary criteria, not even criminal as ordinarily defined—to the frustration of the government agents. This man represents instead a new phenomenon that is quasi-criminal, quasi-psychotic due to possession by the archetype of the Apocalypse. And that means, since a human ego has been bypassed, that the possessed individual is functioning "inhumanly." It is by that very fact a psychological state that generates charisma with tremendous energy in it! Melville gives us an extraordinarily accurate picture of the phenomenon in the figure of Captain Ahab in *Moby-Dick*. In outer history, Hitler is the outstanding example of the same psychological phenomenon writ really large. He was simultaneously "beast and savior," a savior for his friends and a beast for his enemies; and he, too, thought of himself in religious terms.

Appendix II
The Heaven's Gate Cult[5]

The fate of the group called "Heaven's Gate" and their leaders represents yet another manifestation of possession by the Apocalypse archetype: these thirty-nine people said they committed collective suicide in March, 1997, in order to ascend to Heaven—in the manner of a self-willed Rapture—to escape the terrible end of the world. Technically, they were pre-tribulationists, believing that the chosen ones would be "caught up" prior to the fires of Armageddon. And that fact (whether or not the group was aware of it) may account for their peaceful and rather private behavior which did not provoke a fiery confrontation with government as did the Branch Davidians. Nevertheless, the leaders of Heaven's Gate did believe that they would be martyred by the Beast from the abyss and wondered that the world paid them so little attention; the male leader Marshall Applewhite, having waited twenty-four years for this outcome, considered provoking the powers of government to bring it about but chose instead the more introverted solution of suicide. This solution was also decidedly unbiblical; and death by one's own hand is not sanctioned by Christian theology.

Here we meet the interesting fact that the Heaven's Gate group did and did not fit the materials of the New Testament Book of Revelation. They did fit the "pattern" or the archetype, however, and prove Jung's point that "archetypes are not determined as regards their content, but only as regards their form" yet to be "filled out with the material of conscious experience"[6]. When the group's leaders, Bonnie Nettles and Marshall Applewhite, became possessed by the archetype of the Apocalypse around 1972, they identified with the "two witnesses" of Revelation 11, where we read:

> "But I shall send my two witnesses to prophesy for twelve hundred and sixty days, wearing sackcloth. These are the two olive trees and the two lamps in attendance on the Lord of the world. Fire comes from their mouths and consumes their enemies if anyone tries to harm them; and anyone who tries to harm them will certainly be killed in this way. They have the power to lock up the sky so that it does not rain as long as they are prophesying; they have the power to turn water into blood and strike the whole world with any plague as often as they like. When they have completed their witnessing, the beast that comes out of the Abyss is coming to make war on them and overcome them and kill them. Their corpses lie in the main street of the great city known by the symbolic names Sodom and Egypt, in which their Lord was crucified. People of every race, tribe, language and nation stare at their corpses, for three-and-a-half days, not letting them be buried, and the people of the world are glad about it and celebrate the event by giving presents to each other, because these two prophets have been a plague to the people of the world."
>
> After the three-and-a-half days, God breathed life into them and they stood up on their feet, and everybody who saw it happen was terrified; then I heard a loud voice from heaven say to them, "Come up here," and while their enemies were watching, they went up to heaven in a cloud. (11:3–12)

In a letter of 1973, Applewhite wrote after a sojourn of several months:

> The time in the "wilderness" has finally ended. During that time I learned the meaning of seperation [sic] from all attachments, concepts, posessions [sic], passions & even self. Jesus' words and example took on their true meaning, and after much necessary suffering—the "Big Daddy" revealed to Bonnie and me our mission. We are his 2 lampstands or candlesticks, his 2 olive trees.[7]

Here we observe a thorough identification with a content of the Book of Revelation although curiously lacking the destructive powers associated with the "two witnesses"—powers that apparently remained unconscious, but which would manifest themselves as the absolute obedience required of their followers even unto death. When arrested for credit card fraud and rental car theft, "The Two"—thoroughly dehumanized—would argue that the Lord of scripture comes as a "thief in the night." In another letter, Applewhite wrote: "Ok, brace yourself for some hard facts, Our Father is NOT the 'sweet' and loving Father in the ways we thought."[8] In agreement with the Book of Revelation the members of Heaven's Gate believed in the imminent Second Coming and even held the somewhat obscure belief of Revelation that the human race is the Lord's "gardening" experiment. *Newsweek* reported their view that:

> Once upon a time, the gods created a physical "Kingdom of Heaven" somewhere among the sky's more visible heavenly bodies. On instructions from the gods, these Kingdom dwellers "planted" humans as a gardening experiment on planet Earth. From time to time, "Representatives" of the Kingdom would make "soul deposits" in these human plants, preparing them for transplanting to what Do called "the Level above Human." When harvest time arrived—at the end of an "age"—a Representative would usurp a human body, instruct a band of the elect and take them back to their interplanetary heaven.[9]

While actually biblical, this statement is also obviously a product of modern science fiction—both of which are ultimately products of the psyche, expressing the Apocalypse archetype. We find in this example of the archetype's "devouring" of human egos a certain freedom of interpretation of the Bible (Nettles was raised a Baptist, Applewhite a Presbyterian minister's son) whereby the "two witnesses" rename themselves more anonymously as "The Two" or—more playfully—as "Guinea and Pig," "Bo and Peep," or as notes of the musical scale, "Do and Ti." The resurrection "cloud" in Revelation was interpreted by Heaven's Gate in modern fashion as a UFO or a spaceship guided by superior alien beings who lived, yes, in the "Kingdom of God" but more accurately and less emotionally in "The Level Above Human."

Psychologically, this group expected and even hoped for the arrival of "alien" contents from the unconscious psyche which

would introduce them to the "next level" of psychological achievement. But they were unconsciously possessed by the archetype of
that realization and were thus unable to see what was actually at
stake. Nettles, Applewhite, and their followers—who would signifi-
cantly number forty in all—were driven by a concrete (and, therefore, destructive) acting out of an inner process that intends to be
creative. It followed "logically" that Ti, who unexpectedly died of
cancer in 1985, was coming back in a spaceship in the wake of the
newly-discovered huge comet Hale-Bopp to gather up her partner
Do and their flock. As if it were the miraculous "star" witnessed by
the wise men of the Gospels 2,000 years ago, the comet became the
"marker" that encouraged Applewhite, now sixty-six years old and
apparently failing, "to take things into our own hands."

As we did with Vernon Howell, we might wonder about the personal reality behind all this impersonal archetypal activity. The leaders of Heaven's Gate—Bonnie Nettles and Marshall Applewhite—
were born in Texas, respectively in 1927 and 1932, of Christian par-
ents. Each married conventionally in their early twenties, each had
children; they began respectable successful careers—the one in
nursing and the other in music. But nurse Nettles showed signs in
the turbulent 1970s of not fitting in with her southern Baptist
upbringing: she embraced fortune telling and astrology, and even
had regular telepathic conversations with a deceased nineteenth-
century monk called "Brother Francis." During this same period,
Applewhite, a professor of voice, began to waver emotionally—
being hospitalized at one point presumably over the conflict of
being homosexual or bisexual in a society (and a Christian family)
that could not accept such realities. And yet, as if in compensation
for such suffering, he had a vision in which he felt he had been
given a "private tutorial by the Lord." A friend reports, "He said a
presence had given him all the knowledge of where the human race
had come from and where it was going."[10] In 1972, the recently-
divorced Nettles who was familiar with spirits met Applewhite who
had been divorced for years but had only recently encountered the
spirit world: And the two became—after some traveling together—
"The Two" of Revelation.

It seems clear that the dissolution of the "container" of traditional religion (Protestant Christianity) had its effect upon the personalities of Bonnie Nettles and Marshall Applewhite. The container could no longer contain them as actual human beings who were groping, however ineffectually, toward a new aeon with new contents; and the religious energies of their souls—activated by awkward personal circumstances if not perhaps by their destinies—spilled into inadequate tributaries. Their identification with those energies, however, gave them an irrational attraction for their followers. The daughter of Nettles reports that after The Two's initial journey together: "They were like magnets . . . . They had this unbelievable power. Suddenly, I felt privileged to be around them."[11] Dick Joslyn, a one-time member of Heaven's Gate, had the same reaction when he met The Two at a meeting: "I know you're not con artists. . . . That means, either you're who you say you are, or you're absolutely mad."[12] Writers of a book performed voice-stress tests on the leaders and concluded that there was no deliberate deception, that they "believed what they were saying." But these personal conclusions make it all the more tragic that our culture lacks a sufficient category—a psychological category—in which to place such aberrant behavior as that of Heaven's Gate. Possession by the archetype of the Apocalypse, however, provides an explanation.

Notes

PREFACE

1. Jung, *Aion, CW* 9.ii, par. 77.

2. Edinger, *An American Jungian*, part 1, videocassette.

3. Edinger, "Ralph Waldo Emerson," pp. 77–99.

4. See Edinger, works cited.

5. Jung, *Aion, CW* 9.ii, par. 282.

6. Edinger, *The Aion Lectures*, p. 135.

7. Edinger, "In Conversation with Edward F. Edinger," p. 165.

8. Edinger, *Transformation of the God-Image*.

9. See Edinger, *The New God-Image*, *Goethe's "Faust"*, and *The Creation of Consciousness*.

10. Edinger, letter made available to the Editor dated May, 1995.

11. David Gonzalez, "Day 17 at Blast Site: Hope Ends and Healing Begins," *New York Times*, May 6th, 1995. Reverend Graham made this statement at the Oklahoma City Memorial Service, April 23rd, 1995, broadcast by CNN.

12. Gilmour, "The Revelation to John," in *The Interpreter's One-Volume Commentary on the Bible*, p. 945.

13. McGinn, "Revelation," in *The Literary Guide to the Bible*, 523.

CHAPTER 1

1. Jung, *Psychology and Religion, CW* 11, par. 557.

2. For an overview of apocalyptic literature in the history of religions see Collins, "Apocalypse," in *The Encyclopedia of Religion*. See also Cohn, *Cosmos, Chaos and the World To Come* (EDITOR).

3. See Appendix 2, "The Heaven's Gate Cult," where the symbolism of the Book of Revelation and science fiction are mixed in a tragic way (EDITOR).

4. See Appendix 1 for "A Case History of Possession by the Apocalypse Archetype: David Koresh" (EDITOR).

5. Technically, these are "post-tribulationists" who believe, contrary to most fundamentalist Christians, that there will not be a safe "rapture" into heaven prior to the terrors of the End. Instead, as Bernard McGinn explains, these Christians preach a "survivalist strategy of building bomb shelters, stockpiling food, preparing alternate energy sources, and military training to protect one's food supply for the coming dark days of Antichrist's rule before the rapture." See McGinn, *Antichrist,* p. 261 (EDITOR).

6. The Jehovah's Witnesses are a distinctly American Christian sect founded in the late nineteenth century. They are convinced, from reading the Bible, that God's true name is "Jehovah" and that his followers are not to be called Christians but "Witnesses." They are further convinced that the End of time is near, and that Jehovah's Witnesses have a particularly clear view of that event from their "Watchtower," the name of the sect's main publication. The Seventh Day Adventists are related to this somewhat more recent apocalyptic sect by way of their connection with William Miller of the mid-nineteenth century American "Millerites." He announced the Advent of Christ and subsequent End of time to be 1843, a date soon rejected by himself and his followers in light of historical events; but his view that Saturday, the "seventh day" of the week, was the true Sabbath—in agreement with Judaism—remained unscathed. For further reading, see Stroup, "Jehovah's Witnesses," in *The Encyclopedia of Religion,* vol. 7. See also Butler and Numbers, "Seventh-Day Adventism," in the same publication, vol. 13 (EDITOR)

7. Edinger writes the following in "An Outline of Analytical Psychology," p. 4:

> Usually the shadow, as indicated by the word, contains inferior characteristics and weaknesses which the ego's self-esteem will not permit it to recognize. . . . So long as the shadow is projected, the individual can hate and condemn freely the weakness and evil he sees in others, while maintaining his own sense of righteousness. Discovery of the shadow as a personal content may, if it is sudden, cause temporary confusion and depression.

See also von Franz, "The Process of Individuation," in Jung, *Man and His Symbols,* especially pp. 171–185 where she discusses the "realization of the shadow" (EDITOR).

8. Edinger says the following, ibid., pp. 7–8:

> The *Self* expresses psychic wholeness or totality. . . . The term mandala is used to describe the representations of the Self, the archetype of totality. The typical mandala in its simplest form is a quadrated circle combining the elements of a circle with a center plus a square, a cross or some other expression of fourfoldness. . . . A fully developed mandala usually emerges in an individual's dreams only after a long process of psychological development. It is then experienced as a release from an otherwise irreconcilable conflict and may convey a numinous awareness of life as something ultimately harmonious and meaningful in spite of its apparent contradictions.

See also von Franz, ibid., for a rich discussion of the Self, pp. 207–254 (EDITOR).

9. The following material relies upon the *NIV Compact Dictionary of the Bible,* pp. 504f.

10. Here is where fundamentalist "prophecy" concerning our current situation belongs. The author is stating that a connection really does exist between a literal interpretation of scripture and psychology and that there is a contemporary "hook" for the fundamentalist Christian projection of a concrete End (EDITOR).

11. Jung writes: "For my private use I call the sphere of paradoxical existence, i.e., the instinctive unconscious, the Pleroma [Greek, 'that which fills', 'the fullness'], a term borrowed from Gnosticism." See *Letters,* vol. 1, p. 61 (EDITOR).

12. See the classic study by R.H. Charles, *The Revelation of St. John,* two volumes, in *The International Critical Commentary.*

13. von Franz, *Aurora Consurgens.*

14. Jung, *Mysterium Coniunctionis, CW* 14, par. 521.

15. Ford, *Revelation,* in *The Anchor Bible,* pp. 28ff.

16. Jung, *Answer to Job, CW* 11, par. 698.

17. Ibid., par. 730–32.

18. Jung, *Mysterium, CW* 14, par. 209.

19. Jung, *The Archetypes and the Collective Unconscious, CW* 9.i, par. 217. See also Edinger, *Ego and Archetype,* p. 69.

CHAPTER 2

1. See figure 0.1. The noun "numinosum" is used commonly by Jungians and scholars of religion. It derives from the adjective "numinous," coined by Rudolf Otto in his great work *Das Heilige* (Breslau, 1917) translated into English with the somewhat inaccurate title, *Idea of the Holy.* These terms refer to divine reality regardless of tradition; the Latin background is *numen*—"nod, the divine nod of approval, or divinity." Thus, something "numinous" is "full of the divine," fraught with the awareness and feeling of being in the presence of sacred reality (EDITOR).

2. The author has defined this psychotherapeutic technique in "An Outline of Analytical Psychology," p. 11: "Active imagination is a process of conscious, deliberate participation in fantasy. It often takes the form of a dialogue between the ego and a fantasy figure—perhaps the shadow or anima. It can be extremely helpful in bringing an unconscious content into consciousness especially when the ego feels it has reached an impasse" (EDITOR).

3. Zechariah reports:

As I look, there is a lamp-stand entirely of gold with a bowl at the top of it; it holds seven lamps, with seven openings for the lamps on it. . . . The angel who was talking to me replied, "Do you not know what they are?" I said, "No, my lord." He then gave me this answer, "These seven are the eyes of Yahweh, which range over the whole world." (Zechariah 4:2–10)

Unless otherwise stated, all biblical references are to the New Jerusalem Bible.

4. Jung, *Answer to Job* in *Psychology and Religion, CW* 11, par. 579n.

5. For a thorough treatment of alchemical terms and their relationship to psychology, see Edinger, *Anatomy of the Psyche* (EDITOR).

6. See Jung's dream of the psyche as a "multi-level house" in Jung, *Memories, Dreams, Reflections,* pp. 158f. (EDITOR).

7. Jung, *Memories,* p. 297.

8. Jung, *Letters,* vol. 1, p. 298. Von Franz, *Projection and Re-Collection,* p. 177.

9. Jung, *Letters,* vol. 2, pp. 218–19.

10. Jung, *Symbols of Transformation, CW* 5, par. 524. See also Edinger, *Tranformation of Libido,* Epigraph and p. 60 where the author states: "There are certain places in Jung's works where he lays things out with utmost clarity. If you understand this paragraph thoroughly, you will understand Jungian psychology" (EDITOR).

11. Ford, *Revelation,* p. 388.

12. Ibid., p. 79.

13. Jung, *Psychology and Alchemy, CW* 12, pars. 67f. *Symbols of Transformation, CW* 5; e.g., pars. 289 and 296.

14. A popular American movie, *Raiders of the Lost Ark,* the first of an "Indiana Jones Trilogy," exploits this motif (EDITOR).

15. Jung, *Civilization in Transition, CW* 10, par. 583.

16. See Jung, *Mysterium Coniunctionis, CW* 14, par. 670, where he describes *unio mentalis* as "the interior oneness which today we call individuation."

17. The author explores this significant idea at some length in his work, *The Creation of Consciousness,* pp. 23ff. (EDITOR).

18. Zeller, *The Dream,* p. 2. See also Zeller, "The Task of the Analyst," in *Psychological Perspectives,* p. 75. This dream is quoted in Edinger, *The Creation of Consciousness,* p. 11.

19. Ibid.

20. Jung, "Is Analytical Psychology a Religion?," in *C.G. Jung Speaking,* p. 97.

21. Jung, *The Development of Personality, CW* 17, par. 309. Edinger, *The Christian Archetype,* p. 53.

22. See Koenig, "Hospitality," in *The Encyclopedia of Religion* (EDITOR).

23. As this chapter was being put in final draft, the newspapers reported the suicide deaths of 39 persons in California who belonged to an apocalyptic group called "Heaven's Gate." They died deliberately to avoid Armageddon and enter the Kingdom of Heaven, enacting concretely the archetype of "Rapture." See Appendix 2 (EDITOR).

CHAPTER 3

1. "Anointing" with oil or ointment in the ancient world was a ritual activity conferring sacrality (i.e. providing the power and authority associated with the sacred) to exceptional stones or trees, to priests, prophets, and kings. The psychological point seems to be that what is given in nature is not yet complete, that "something sacred" needs to be *added* to the ordinary ego to give it the power and authority to stand out, to prophesy, and to rule: that something is the energy of the Self archetype at the core of the psyche (EDITOR).

2. Perry, *Lord of the Four Quarters.*

3. *The Apocryphon of John,* p. 107.

4. Edinger, *The Mysterium Lectures,* pp. 164f.

5. Eliot, *Collected Poems,* p. 89.

6. See Edinger, *The Mysterium Lectures,* pp. 145ff. See also his work, *The Bible and the Psyche,* pp. 124ff. (EDITOR).

7. Astrologers break down the broad sweep of history into periods of roughly two thousand years, each of which is influenced by its sign of the zodiac. Thus, the period just prior to the time of Christ is designated as the "Age of Aries," whose symbol is the ram; while the birth of Christ inaugurates the "Age of Pisces," symbolized by two fish. We, then, are either in or about to enter the "Age of Aquarius." The author's point is that Christ is on the threshold between two aeons. He is thus both the Ram of the old aeon and the first Fish of the new aeon (EDITOR).

8. Jung, *Answer to Job, CW* 11, par. 708.

9. Jung, *Mysterium Coniunctionis, CW* 14, par. 4. The editors of the English version of Jung's *Collected Works* did not capitalize the term "Self." In German, all nouns are capitalized. Jung's wishes are clear, however. In his letters, *written in English,* he capitalized the term. See Jung, *Letters,* vol. 1, p. 427, and vol. 2, p. 571.

10. Judah is a lion's whelp;
　　You stand over your prey, my son.
　　Like a lion he crouches and lies down,
　　a mighty lion; who dare rouse him?

11. Jung, *Aion, CW* 9.ii, pars. 167f.

12. Edinger, *The Creation of Consciousness,* pp. 35ff. See also Elder, *The Body,* chapter 5 on "The Eye."

13. Hill, *Dreaming the End of the World,* p. 67.

14. Ibid., p. 83.

15. Jung, *Psychology and Religion, CW* 11, pars. 381ff.

16. Ibid., par. 390. See note 9 above.

17. Ibid., par. 397. See note 9 above.

18. Ibid., par. 398. See also Edinger, *Ego and Archetype,* pp. 96ff.

CHAPTER 4

1. Quispel, in his work, *The Secret Book of Revelation,* adds to the list (p. 26): seven thunders, seven heads on the dragon and beast, seven plagues, seven mountains, seven kings, and "probably also seven millennia of world history. John's thought seems to be dominated by this figure. It is by no means impossible that he deliberately divided his book into seven sections, as was assumed to have been the case in the Middle Ages" (EDITOR).

2. Glatzer, *The Essential Philo.*

3. Philo, *On the Account of the World's Creation Given by Moses,* XXX–XXXIII.

4. See Westcott, *Numbers: Their Occult Power and Mystic Virtues* (1890); reprinted as *The Occult Power of Numbers.*

5. The seven "planets" were, in their classical acceptance and order of distance from the earth: Moon, Mercury, Venus, Sun, Mars, Jupiter, and Saturn (EDITOR).

6. Jung, *Psychology and Alchemy, CW* 12, par. 82.

7. Edinger, *Ego and Archetype,* chapter 7.

8. Jung, *Mysterium Coniunctionis, CW* 14, par. 8. Jung reports on an alchemical treatise as follows:

> The text gives the following diagram (see figure 4.1). B C D E represent the outside, A is the inside, "as it were the origin and source from which the other letters flow, and likewise the final goal to which they flow back," FG stands for Above and Below. "Together the letters A B C D E F G clearly signify the hidden magical Septenary." The central point A, the origin and goal, the "Ocean or great sea," is also called a *circulus exiguus,* very small circle, and a "mediator making peace between the enemies or elements, that they may love one another in a meet embrace." This inner circle corresponds to the Mercurial Fountain in the *Rosarium,* which I have described in my "Psychology of the Transference."

See also Jung, *The Psychology of the Transference* in *The Practice of Psychotherapy, CW* 16, pars. 402f.

9. Jung writes in *Psychology and Alchemy, CW* 12, par. 26: "we come to one of the central axioms of alchemy, namely the saying of Maria Prophetissa: 'One becomes two, two becomes three, and out of the third comes the one as the fourth.'" For a discussion of how the three relatively differentiated functions of consciousness can be joined by the inferior fourth function to create the "one" of psychological wholeness, see Jung, *The Phenomenology of the Spirit in Fairytales* in *The Archetypes and the Collective Unconscious, CW* 9.i., pars. 430f. (EDITOR).

10. Compare the tenth avatar or final manifestation of the Hindu god Viṣṇu named Kalkin (Sanskrit, *kalka,* "filthy residue") who will arrive at the end of this sinful Kali Age "in the form of a man mounted on a white horse, with a flaming sword in his hand. He will judge the wicked, reward the good, and restore the age of gold"—as described by Basham, *The Wonder that was India,* p. 307. This image may have been influenced by Christianity or by Zoroastrianism (EDITOR).

11. The morning after government agents attacked the Branch Davidians at Waco, Texas—killing six—their leader David Koresh announced, "we are in the fifth seal." He seemed to mean, as scripture says, "in a little longer" there would be more killings. The scholar James D. Tabor writes: "In other words, the FBI inadvertently played the part of the Babylonian forces throughout, validating in every detail, to both Koresh and his followers, this chiliastic interpretation of the standoff." See Tabor's essay, "Religious Discourse and Failed Negotiations" in *Armageddon in Waco*, p. 271. See also Appendix 1 in this volume: "A Case History of Possession by the Apocalypse Archetype: David Koresh" (EDITOR).

12. Jung, *Answer to Job*, in *Psychology and Religion*, *CW* 11, par. 641.

13. Virgil, *The Aeneid*, in *Eclogues, Georgics, Aeneid I–VI*, Loeb Classical Library (1935), 241.

14. See Edinger's unpublished letter on this topic in the Editor's Preface (EDITOR).

15. Jung, *Answer to Job*, in *Psychology and Religion*, *CW* 11, par. 708.

16. Ibid., pars. 730–32.

17. Jung, *Alchemical Studies*, *CW* 13, par. 335.

18. Edinger, *Creation of Consciousness*, p. 28.

19. Edinger, *Anatomy of the Psyche*, p. 90.

20. Ford, *Revelation*, pp. 122f.

21. Edinger, *Ego and Archetype*, chapter 9.

22. Ford, *Revelation*, p. 127.

23. Pascal, *Pascal's Pensées*, no. 552, p. 148.

24. See Jonas, *The Gnostic Religion*, p. 228f. For the application of this image to a particular case, see also Edinger, *The Living Psyche*, p. 49 (EDITOR).

CHAPTER 5

1. Ford, *Revelation*, pp. 135–36

2. Jung, *A Study in the Process of Individuation* in *The Archetypes and the Collective Unconscious*, *CW* 9.i, pars. 525ff.

3. Leonard Bernstein, *Mass: A Theatre Piece for Singers, Players, and Dancers*, 1971.

4. Edinger, *The Mystery of the Coniunctio*, pp. 15f.

5. Ford, *Revelation*, p. 147.

6. Gaer, *The Lore of the Old Testament*, p.221, as cited in Edinger, *The Bible and the Psyche*, p. 85.

7. von Franz, *C.G. Jung: His Myth in Our Time*, p. 174.

8. Ford, *Revelation*, 150.

9. Ibid., pp. 154–55.

10. Edinger, *The Bible and the Psyche,* pp. 49f.

11. Hill, *Dreaming the End of the World,* 81.

12. See Elder, *The Body,* on the symbolism of the "Respiratory and Digestive Systems," chapter 8 (EDITOR).

CHAPTER 6

1. See p. 33.

2. Jung, *Answer to Job* in *Psychology and Religion, CW* 11, par. 711.

3. Ibid., par. 712.

4. Ibid., par. 713.

5. Ibid.

6. Milton, *Paradise Lost.*

7. Kluger, *Satan in the Old Testament.*

8. The author has written in *Goethe's "Faust": Notes for a Jungian Commentary,* p. 14:

> In the sixteenth century the God-image fell out of heaven (metaphysical projection) and landed in the human psyche. In the course of this transition from heaven to earth it undergoes an enantiodromia from Christ to Antichrist. This event paves the way for Faust's encounter with Mephistopheles. . . . Of course the artists, scholars, explorers, reformers and scientists of the sixteenth century did not consider their activities as devilish. They were all good Christians, they thought, who were excited by the expansion of human knowledge and energy. But things looked different from the standpoint of the unconscious which, like a compensating dream, generated the Faust legend.

> The relevant comment by Jung is in *Aion, CW* 9.ii, par. 78:

> The ideal of spirituality striving for the heights was doomed to clash with the materialistic earth-bound passion to conquer matter and master the world. This change became visible at the time of the "Renaissance" (EDITOR).

9. Edinger, *Encounter with the Self: A Jungian Commentary on William Blake's "Illustrations of the Book of Job",* pp. 54ff.

10. Hill, p. 84.

11. Jung, *Aion, CW* 9.ii, par. 178.

12. Edinger, *The Bible and the Psyche,* p. 159.

13. Patai, *The Messiah Texts,* pp. 238–39.

14. Ibid., pp. 252–53.

15. Jung, *Mysterium Coniunctionis, CW* 14, par. 52.

16. Ford, *Revelation,* p. 216.

17. McGinn notes that fundamentalist Christians have been less fascinated with Hitler as the bearer of "666" than with Mussolini who made claims to restore a Roman Empire that historically persecuted Christianity. He adds to the "flypaper" list Pope John Paul II, Henry Kissinger, Mikhail Gorbachev (with that suspicious red mark on his head), Ronald Wilson Reagan (whose three names each have six letters, a modern simpler variation on alphabet-numerical equivalence), Pat Robertson (with his glib style of a false prophet), and Saddam Hussein. *Antichrist,* pp. 256ff. (EDITOR).

18. Edinger, *Ego and Archetype,* chapter 7.

19. Ibid.

CHAPTER 7

1. Jung, *Answer to Job* in *Psychology and Religion, CW* 11, par. 719.

2. Ibid., par. 733.

3. Jung, *Mysterium Coniunctionis, CW* 14, par. 192.

4. Charles, *Apocrypha and Pseudepigrapha of the Old Testament in English,* vol. 2, p. 192.

5. Jung, *Answer to Job* in *Psychology and Religion, CW* 11, par. 669.

6. Edinger, *The Creation of Consciousness,* p. 28. The dream is discussed also by von Franz in *Projection and Re-collection in Jungian Psychology,* p. 112.

7. *The Gospel of Thomas,* p. 127.

8. Hill, p. 82.

9. See Jung's boyhood dream: "I saw before me the cathedral, the blue sky. God sits on his golden throne, high above the world—and from under the throne an enormous turd falls upon the sparkling new roof, shatters it, and breaks the walls of the cathedral asunder." *Memories, Dreams, Reflections,* pp. 36ff.

10. Jung, *Nietzsche's "Zarathustra",* p. 255f.

11. Hill, p. 120.

CHAPTER 8

1. Lucretius, *Of the Nature of Things,* I.1-25. See also Edinger, *The Eternal Drama,* pp. 46ff, where the poem is discussed.

2. Jung, *Symbols of Transformation, CW* 5, par. 104.

3. Jung, *Mysterium Coniunctionis, CW* 14, pars. 368–463.

4. Ibid., par. 423.

5. Ibid., pars. 426f.

6. Jung, *Psychology and Alchemy*, *CW* 12, par. 138.

7. Ibid., par. 139.

8. Augustine, *The City of God*.

9. See Hegel's *Lectures on the Philosophy of History*, translated as *Reason in History*.

CHAPTER 9

1. See Speight, "Creeds: An Overview," in *The Encyclopedia of Religion*, vol. 4, pp. 138ff.

2. Technically, Christianity claims that a person is judged by God 1) at every moment and reaps during that person's lifetime (albeit inscrutably) rewards for good acts and punishments for evil ones. But 2), at death, a more definitive judgment occurs as the body decays in the grave and the soul either ascends to heaven or descends to hell (for some Christians, an "intermediate state" of purgatory is also possible). As Augustine explains, however, this judgment upon death is merely a "foretaste" of 3) the absolute and eternal justice which will occur at the Last Judgment after the resurrection of all dead bodies at the world's end. See Elder, *Body*, pp. 135f, 417f. (EDITOR).

3. Brandon, *The Judgment of the Dead*.

4. Handel, *Messiah* (1742).

5. Edinger, *The Living Psyche*, p. 29.

6. Plato, *The Republic*, p. 839.

7. Ibid., *Gorgias*, p. 303f.

8. Jung, *Memories, Dreams, Reflections*, p. 291.

9. Jung, *The Psychology of the Transference* in *The Practice of Psychotherapy*, *CW* 16, pars. 402ff. See his figures 2 and 3.

10. *The Aeneid of Virgil, Edited by John Dryden*, pp. 198f.

12. *Larousse Encyclopedia of Mythology*, pp. 41f.

13. See Elder, *Body*, "Weighing of the Heart," 298ff. (EDITOR).

14. Emerson, "Compensation," p. 181.

15. Ibid.

16. Jung, *Memories, Dreams, Reflections*, p. 345.

CHAPTER 10

1. Jung, *Memories, Dreams, Reflections*, p. 176.

2. Jung, *Answer to Job* in *Psychology and Religion*, *CW* 11, par. 727.

3. Ibid., par. 728.

4. Edinger, *The Creation of Consciousness*, pp. 28f.

5. Jung, *Answer to Job* in *Psychology and Religion, CW* 11, par. 660.

6. Edinger, *Transformation of the God-Image*, pp. 80f.

7. Origen, *On First Principles*, p. 52. See Edinger, *The Aion Lectures*, for additional discussion of *apocatastasis*, pp. 46ff.

8. Jung, *Letters*, vol. 2, p. 239.

9. Jung, *Answer to Job* in *Psychology and Religion, CW* 11, par. 740.

10. Emerson, *Nature*, p. 3.

11. Jung, *Answer to Job* in *Psychology and Religion, CW* 11, par. 659.

12. Ibid., pars. 746f.

13. Jung, *Letters*, vol. 2, p. 213.

14. Jung, *Answer to Job* in *Psychology and Religion, CW* 11, par. 747.

15. Jung, *The Undiscovered Self* in *Civilization in Transition, CW* 10, par. 585.

16. Hill, *Dreaming the End of the World*, pp. 137f.

17. Jung, *Mysterium Coniunctionis, CW* 14, par. 209.

18. Jung, *Letters*, vol. 2, par. 239.

APPENDICES

1. See the author's unpublished letter on the topic of "terrorism" in the Editor's Preface (EDITOR).

2. See Breault and King, *Inside the Cult.*

3. Although Christians, the Seventh Day Adventists believe themselves to be spiritual descendents of David, the ideal king of Israel, based upon the scripture in Isaiah 11.1f: "A shoot [or branch] will spring from the stock of Jesse, a new shoot will grow from his roots. On him will rest the spirit of Yahweh" — which shoot or branch is identified as Jesus Christ. When a reform movement developed within the denomination in 1929, they simply called themselves "Davidians" to distinguish themselves from other Seventh Day Adventists. When an even more radical reform developed among the Davidians in 1955 (due in part to failed prophecies of the end of the world), they took on the distinctive name of "Branch Davidians," terminology which does not deny their Seventh Day Adventist heritage. It was with this group that Vernon Howell made contact, in Texas, in 1981. See Pitts, "Davidians and Branch Davidians: 1929-1987" in *Armageddon in Waco*, chapter 2 (EDITOR).

4. Breault and King, *Inside the Cult*, p. 1. Consult Isaiah 45.1ff:

Thus says Yahweh
to his anointed one,
to Cyrus whom, he says,

I have grasped by his right hand,
to make the nations bow before him

5. Written by the Editor with Dr. Edinger's approval.

6. Jung, *CW* 9.i., par. 155.

7. Barry Bearak, "Eyes on Glory: Pied Pipers of Heaven's Gate," *New York Times,* 28 April 1997, p. 1.

8. Ibid., p. 10.

9. Kenneth L. Woodward, "Christ and Comets," *Newsweek,* April 7, 1997, p. 41.

10. Bearak, *New York Times,* p. 10.

11. Ibid.

12. Ibid., p. 11. This same reasoning has been used to verify Jesus' claim to be the son of God: either he was (1) a con artist and a liar, (2) crazy, or (3) telling the truth. (4) The fourth possibility is that his sincere, "truthful," conviction derived from identification with the archetype.

Bibliography

The Apocryphon of John. Translated by Fredrik Wisse. In *The Nag Hammadi Library* (San Francisco: Harper and Row, 1988), edited by James M. Robinson, pp. 104–123.

Augustine. *The City of God.* Translated by Marcus Dods. New York: Modern Library/Random House, 1950.

Basham, A.L. *The Wonder that Was India.* New York: Grove Press, 1954.

Bernstein, Leonard. *Mass: A Theatre Piece for Singers, Players, and Dancers,* 1971.

Brandon, S.G.F. *The Judgment of the Dead: The Idea of Life After Death in the Major Religions.* New York: Scribner's, 1967.

Breault, Marc, and Martin King. *Inside the Cult.* New York: Signet Press/Penguin Books, 1993.

Butler, Jonathan M., and Ronald L. Numbers. "Seventh-Day Adventism." In Eliade, *The Encyclopedia of Religion,* vol. 13, pp. 179–183.

Charles, R.H. *Apocrypha and Pseudepigrapha of the Old Testament in English.* 2 vols. 1913. Reprint, Oxford: Oxford University Press, 1969.

———. *The Revelation of St. John,* 2 vols. In *The International Critical Commentary,* edited by S.R. Driver, et al. (Edinburgh: T and T Clark, 1920).

Cohn, Norman. *Cosmos, Chaos, and the World to Come: The Ancient Roots of Apocalyptic Faith.* New Haven: Yale University Press, 1993.

Collins, John J. "Apocalypse: An Overview." In Eliade, *The Encyclopedia of Religion,* vol. 1, 334–36.

CNN. Televised coverage of the "Oklahoma City Memorial Service," 23 April 1995.

Edinger, Edward F. *The Aion Lectures: Exploring the Self in C.G. Jung's "Aion".* Edited by Deborah A. Wesley. Toronto: Inner City Books, 1996.

———. *An American Jungian: Edward F. Edinger in Conversation with Lawrence Jaffe.* Part 1, "Personal Life and Development." Videocassette produced and directed by Dianne D. Cordic, 1991.

———. *Anatomy of the Psyche: Alchemical Symbolism in Psychotherapy.* La Salle, Illinois: Open Court, 1985.

------. *The Bible and the Psyche: Individuation Symbolism in the Old Testament.* Toronto: Inner City Books, 1986.

------. *The Christian Archetype: A Jungian Commentary on the Life of Christ.* Toronto: Inner City Books, 1987.

------. *The Creation of Consciousness: Jung's Myth for Modern Man.* Toronto: Inner City Books, 1984.

------. *Ego and Archetype: Individuation and the Religious Function of the Psyche.* New York: C.G. Jung Foundation for Analytical Psychology, 1972.

------. *Encounter with the Self: A Jungian Commentary on William Blake's "Illustrations of the Book of Job".* Toronto: Inner City Books, 1986.

------. *The Eternal Drama: The Inner Meaning of Greek Mythology.* Edited by Deborah A. Wesley. Boston: Shambhala, 1994.

------. *Goethe's "Faust": Notes for a Jungian Commentary.* Toronto: Inner City Books, 1990.

------. "In Conversation with Edward F. Edinger." Interview by David Serbin. *Psychological Perspectives* 14 (1983).

------. *The Living Psyche: A Jungian Analysis in Pictures.* Wilmette, Illinois: Chiron, 1990.

------. *Melville's Moby-Dick: An American Nekyia.* 2nd ed. Toronto: Inner City Books, 1995.

------. *The Mysterium Lectures: A Journey through C.G. Jung's "Mysterium Coniunctionis".* Edited by Joan Dexter Blackmer. Toronto: Inner City Books, 1995.

------. *The Mystery of the Coniunctio: Alchemical Image of Individuation.* Edited by Joan Dexter Blackmer. Toronto: Inner City Books, 1994.

------. *The New God-Image: A Study of Jung's Key Letters Concerning the Evolution of the Western God-Image.* Edited by Dianne D. Cordic and Charles Yates. Wilmette, Illinois: Chiron, 1996.

------. "An Outline of Analytical Psychology." *Quadrant* 1 (1968): 1–12.

------. "Ralph Waldo Emerson: Naturalist of the Soul." *Spring* (1965): 77–99.

------. *Transformation of Libido: A Seminar on C.G. Jung's "Symbols of Transformation".* Edited by Dianne D. Cordic. Los Angeles: C.G. Jung Bookstore, 1994.

------. *Transformation of the God-Image: An Elucidation of Jung's "Answer to Job".* Edited by Lawrence W. Jaffe. Toronto: Inner City Books, 1992.

Elder, George R. *The Body: An Encyclopedia of Archetypal Symbolism.* Boston: Shambhala, 1996.

Eliade, Mircea, ed. *The Encyclopedia of Religion.* New York: Macmillan, 1987.

Eliot, T.S. *Collected Poems: 1909–1962.* London: Faber and Faber, 1963.

Emerson, Ralph Waldo. "Compensation." In *The Selected Writings of Ralph Waldo Emerson,* edited by Brooks Atkinson (New York: Modern Library, 1940).

Ford, J. Massyngberde. 'Revelation'. In *The Anchor Bible*. (New York: Doubleday, 1975).

Gaer, Joseph. *The Lore of the Old Testament*. New York: Grosset and Dunlap, 1966.

Gilmour, S. Maclean. "The Revelation to John." In *The Interpreter's One-Volume Commentary on the Bible*, edited by Charles M. Laymon (Nashville: Abingdon Press, 1971), pp. 945–968.

Glatzer, Nahum N. *The Essential Philo*. New York: Schocken, 1971.

Handel, George Frederick. *Messiah*. 1742.

Hegel, G.W.F. *Reason in History: A General Introduction to the Philosophy of History*. Translated by Robert S. Hartman. Indianapolis: Bobbs-Merrill, 1953.

Hill, Michael Ortiz. *Dreaming the End of the World: Apocalypse as a Rite of Passage*. Dallas: Spring Publications, 1994.

Jung, C.G. *C.G. Jung Speaking: Interviews and Encounters*. Edited by William McGuire and R.F.C. Hull. Princeton: Princeton University Press, 1977.

———. *Collected Works*. 20 vols. Princeton: Princeton University Press, 1977.

———. *Letters*. 2 vols. Edited by G. Adler and A. Jaffé. Princeton: Princeton University Press, 1975.

———. *Memories, Dreams, Reflections*. Edited by A. Jaffé. New York: Vintage, 1963.

Jonas, Hans. *The Gnostic Religion*. 2nd ed. Boston: Beacon Press, 1963.

Kluger, Rivkah Schärf. *Satan in the Old Testament*. Translated by Hildegard Nagel. Evanston, Illinois: Northwestern University Press, 1967.

Koenig, John. "Hospitality." In Eliade, *The Encyclopedia of Religion*, vol. 6, pp. 470–73.

LaRousse Encyclopedia of Mythology. Buffalo: Prometheus, 1959.

Lucretius. *Of the Nature of Things*. Translated by W.E. Leonard. New York: Dutton/Everyman Library, 1979.

McGinn, Bernard. *Antichrist: Two Thousand Years of the Human Fascination with Evil*. New York: HarperCollins, 1994.

———. "Revelation." In *The Literary Guide to the Bible*, edited by Robert Alter and Frank Kermode (Cambridge, Mass.: The Belknap Press of Harvard University Press, 1987), pp. 523–541.

Milton, John. *Paradise Lost: A Poem in Twelve Books*. Edited by Merritt Y. Hughes. Indianapolis: Bobbs-Merrill, 1962.

New York Times, 6 May 1995 and 28 April 1997.

NIV Compact Dictionary of the Bible. Edited by J.D. Douglas and Merrill C. Tenney. Grand Rapids: Zondervan, 1989.

Otto, Rudolf. *Idea of the Holy*. Oxford: Oxford University Press, 1950.

Origen. *On First Principles*. Edited by G.W. Butterworth. New York: Harper and Row, 1966.

Pascal, Blaise. *Pascal's Pensées*. New York: Dutton, 1958.

Patai, Raphael. *The Messiah Texts*. Detroit: Wayne State University Press, 1979.

Perry, John Weir. *Lord of the Four Quarters*. New York: Macmillan, 1966.

Philo. *Philo*. Vol. 1. Loeb Classical Library, 1929.

Pitts, William L., Jr. "Davidians and Branch Davidians: 1929–1987." In Wright, *Armageddon in Waco*, pp. 20–42.

Plato. *The Republic* and *The Gorgias*. In *The Collected Dialogues of Plato: Including the Letters*, edited by Edith Hamilton and Huntington Cairns (Princeton: Princeton University Press, 1961) pp. 575–844 and 229–307.

Quispel, Gilles. *The Secret Book of Revelation*. New York: McGraw-Hill, 1979.

Raiders of the Lost Ark. 115 min. LucasFilm Ltd, 1981.

Speight, R. Marston. "Creeds: An Overview." In Eliade, *The Encylopedia of Religion*, vol. 4, pp. 138–140.

Stroup, Herbert Hewitt. "Jehovah's Witnesses." In Eliade, *The Encyclopedia of Religion*, vol. 7, pp. 564–66.

Tabor, James D. "Religious Discourse and Failed Negotiations." In Wright, *Armageddon in Waco*, pp. 263–281.

Virgil. *The Aeneid of Virgil, Edited by John Dryden*. Edited by Robert Fitzgerald. New York: Macmillan, 1965.

———. *Eclogues, Georgics, Aeneid I-VI*. Loeb Classical Library, 1935.

von Franz, Marie-Louise. *Aurora Consurgens*. New York: Pantheon, 1966.

———. *C.G. Jung: His Myth in Our Time*. Translated by William H. Kennedy. New York: C.G. Jung Foundation for Analytical Psychology, 1975.

———. "The Process of Individuation." In *Man and his Symbols*, edited by C.G. Jung (New York: Dell, 1964), pp. 157–254.

———. *Projection and Re-Collection in Jungian Psychology: Reflections of the Soul*. La Salle, Illinois: Open Court, 1980.

Westcott, W. Wynn. *Numbers: Their Occult Power and Mystic Virtues*. 1890. Reprinted as *The Occult Power of Numbers* (North Hollywood, California: New Castle,1984).

Woodward, Kenneth L. "Christ and Comets." *Newsweek*, April 7th, 1997, pp. 40–43.

Wright, Stuart A., ed. *Armageddon in Waco: Critical Perspectives on the Branch Davidian Conflict*. Chicago: University of Chicago Press, 1995.

Zeller, Max. *The Dream: The Vision of the Night*. Edited by Janet Dallett. Los Angeles: The Analytical Psychology Club of Los Angeles and the C.G. Jung Institute of Los Angeles, 1975.

———. "The Task of the Analyst." *Psychological Perspectives* 6 (Spring 1975).

Permissions

Permission is acknowledged for use of the following illustrations: *Saint John the Evangelist on Patmos* (figure 0.1). The Limbourg Brothers. From *Les Très Riches Heures du Duc de Berry*. Ms. 65/1284, f. 108v. Musée Condé, Chantilly. Giraudon/Art Resource, New York. *Saint John's Vision of Christ and the Seven Candlesticks* (figure 2.1). Albrecht Dürer (1471–1528). Woodcut from *The Revelation of Saint John* (Rev. I, 12–16), 1498 (B. 62) Willi Kurth, *The Complete Woodcuts of Albrecht Dürer*. Dover Pictorial Archive Series (New York: Dover, 1963). *The Key of David and the Open Door* (figure 2.5). Illumination from the *Douce Apocalypse* (Ms. Douce 180, p. 9). 13th century, C.E. Courtesy of the Bodleian Library, Department of Special Collections and Western Manuscripts, University of Oxford. *Agnus Dei* (The Lamb of God) (figure 3.1). 11th–12th century, C.E. Detail from the apse fresco in the Church of Sant Climent de Taüll. Museu Nacional d'Art de Catalunya, Barcelona. *Allegory* (figure 3.2). Jan Provost (1465–1529). 16th century, C.E. Louvre, Paris. Scala/Art Resource, New York. *And my Servant Job shall pray for you* (figure 3.3). William Blake (1757–1827). *Book of Job*, pl. 18. The Pierpont Morgan Library, New York. The Pierpont Morgan Library/Art Resource, New York. Diagram of the alchemical Septenary (figure 4.1). C.G. Jung, *Collected Works of C.G. Jung*, vol. 14. par. 8. Copyright © 1959 by Princeton University Press. Reproduced by permission of Princeton University Press. *The Four Horsemen of the Apocalypse* (figure 4.2). Albrecht Dürer. Woodcut from *The Revelation of Saint John* (Rev. VI, 1–7), 1498. (B. 64) Location not indicated. Foto Marburg/Art Resource, New York. *The Opening of the Fifth and Sixth Seals, the Distribution of White Garments among the Martyrs, and the Fall of Stars* (figure 4.3). Woodcut from *The Revelation of Saint John* (Rev. VII, 1–3). 1498. (B. 65) Kurth, *Complete Woodcuts of Albrecht Dürer. Sealing of the Saints* (figure 4.4). Bible. N.T. German. 1522. *Das Neue Testament Deutzsche*, Wittenberg, 1522, leaf 2b2(v). Courtesy of the Rare Books Division, The New York Public Library; Astor, Lennox, and Tilden Foundations. *Painting by a woman patient* (figure 5.2). C.G. Jung, *Collected Works of C.G. Jung*, vol. 9.i, par. 525 (picture 2). Copyright © 1959 by Princeton University Press. Reprinted by permission of Princeton University Press. *The Abyss is Opened and Locusts Emerge* (figure 5.3). Bible. German, 1543. *Biblia: Das ist: Die gantze Heilige Schriffte . . .* Wittenberg, 1543, leaf CCCXL(r) (*KB+1543). Courtesy of the Rare Books Division, The New York Public Library; Astor, Lenox, and Tilden Foundations. *Saint John Devours the Book God Presented to Him* (figure

5.4). Albrecht Dürer. Woodcut from *The Revelation of Saint John* (Rev. X, 1–5, 8–10). 1498. (B.70) Bibliothèque Nationale, Paris. Giraudon/Art Resource, New York. *A Storm, the Woman, and the Dragon* (figure 6.1). Illumination of Norman manuscript, ca. 1320. *Apocalypse in Latin*. Courtesy of the Metropolitan Museum of Art, New York. The Cloisters Collection, 1968. (68.174 20r). *Behemoth and Leviathan* (figure 6.2). Watercolor from *The Book of Job*. The Pierpont Morgan Library, New York. The Pierpont Morgan Library/Art Resource, New York. *The Fall of Satan* (figure 6.3). William Blake. Watercolor from *The Book of Job*. The Pierpont Morgan Library, New York. The Pierpont Morgan Library/Art Resource, New York. *The Sea Monster and the Beast with the Lamb's Horns* (figure 6.4). Albrecht Dürer. Woodcut from *The Revelation of Saint John* (Rev. XIII, 1013; XIV, 14–17). 1498. (B. 74) Bibliothèque Nationale, Paris. Giraudon/Art Resource, New York. *Marked by the Beast* (figure 6.5). Illumination. Ms. Auct. D.4.14. Fol. 36(v). Courtesy of the Bodleian Library, Oxford. *Hell* (figure 7.1). The Limbourg Brothers. From *Les Très Riches Heures du Duc de Berry*. Ms. 65/1284, f. 108v. Musée Condé, Chantilly. Giraudon/Art Resource, New York. *Dragons Vomiting Frogs* (figure 7.2). Miniature from the *Liber Floridus*, 15th century, C.E. Musée Condé, Chantilly. Giraudon/Art Resource, New York. *The Whore of Babylon* (figure 8.1). William Blake. Watercolor. Courtesy of the Department of Prints and Drawings, British Museum, London. *The Second Angel* [Destruction of Babylon] (figure 8.2). Ilumination from the Norman manuscript, *Apocalypse in Latin*. ca. 1320. Courtesy of the Metropolitan Museum of Art, New York. The Cloisters Collection, 1968 (68.174 26v). *Christ*, detail of *Last Judgment* (figure 9.1). Michelangelo Buonarroti. Sistine Chapel, Vatican Palace, Vatican State. Alinari/Art Resource, New York. *Weighing the Heart* (figure 9.2). Egyptian Antiquities, The British Museum, London. (EA 10470 sheet 3). *The New Jerusalem* (figure 10.1). Gustave Doré (1832–1883). Engraving from *La Sainte Bible* (Rev. XXI, 9–27). 1865 (Plate 241). *The Doré Bible: Illustrations*. Dover Pictorial Archive Series (New York: Dover, 1974).

Index